MW00423530

PRAYER
MINISTRY
VOLUNTEER HANDBOOK

PRAYER
MINISTRY
VOLUNTEER HANDBOOK

Equipping You to Serve

First Edition: Year 2019
Prayer Ministry Volunteer Handbook / Outreach, Inc.
Paperback ISBN: 978-1-946453-77-8
eBook ISBN: 978-1-946453-78-5

CHURCHLEADERS
PRESS

Colorado Springs

PRAYER MINISTRY

VOLUNTEER HANDBOOK

Equipping You to Serve

Written by
David and Kim Butts

General Editor
Mark A. Taylor

CHURCHLEADERS
PRESS

Colorado Springs

CONTENTS

INTRODUCTION

to the *Outreach Ministry Guides* Series

Each of you should use whatever gift you have received to serve others, as faithful stewards of God's grace in its various forms
(1 Peter 4:10).

*T*his handbook is part of a series designed to equip and empower church volunteers for effective ministry. If you're reading this, chances are you're a church volunteer. Thanks for your willingness to serve!

Several things make this handbook unique:

- The content is specific and practical for your given area of ministry.
- The information is compiled by experienced ministry practitioners—folks who've worked, served, and helped to train others in this particular area.
- It's written with you—a ministry volunteer—in mind.

Within these pages, you'll find three sections. The first gives a brief overview of fundamental principles to provide you with a solid foundation for the ministry area in which you're serving.

Section 2 unpacks various roles and responsibilities. Understanding your role and the roles of your fellow teammates helps the ministry team serve together well.

Finally, Section 3 provides a multitude of practical ministry tools. These ideas and tips will help you demonstrate Jesus' love to the people you serve at your church.

Whether you're a first-time volunteer or a seasoned veteran, my prayer is that the information and practical tools in this handbook will encourage and assist you. May God bless and guide you in your ministry!

— **Matt Lockhart,** Project Manager

INTRODUCTION

to the *Prayer Ministry Volunteer Handbook*

*R*ead this book to decide how your prayer ministry should look and what it should seek to accomplish. Use the variety of practical tools and guidelines you'll find here to be more effective in your ministry.

But before all that, read this book and learn how to pray.

The authors, Dave and Kim Butts, have a prayer ministry that spans the globe, but perhaps their most effective work has been with local congregations like yours. They have a passion for prayer and how it can transform a congregation, impact a community, and enliven individual believers. You will pray with more purpose, greater joy, and deeper effectiveness after adopting the approaches to prayer they describe here.

You will see how to lead others to enjoy their own enriched prayer lives, too. Most of all, you will prepare yourself to help your congregation become "a house of prayer for all nations," and watch as God responds in ways you might not have imagined.

Throughout this book, Dave and Kim Butts challenge us to view prayer not as one more church program, but to make prayer flow through every initiative, every activity, and every "department" in our churches.

And yet their advice, while always founded on lofty principle, is consistently usable and real. Start small, they advise. Move slowly. They'll show you how, even as they motivate you never to stop.

If your congregation has already established a prayer ministry, this handbook will give you resources for shaping and growing it. The "Tools" section alone is worth the price of the book.

But you'll do well to start at the beginning. Your prayer life—and your prayer ministry—will likely never be the same.

— **Mark A. Taylor,** General Editor

SECTION 1

PRAYER MINISTRY FOUNDATIONS

*T*he content found in this Section provides you with the biblical basis and fundamental principles of a prayer ministry. Knowing and understanding the role of prayer will help equip and empower you as you participate in the prayer ministry at your church.

CHAPTER 1

THE SCRIPTURAL BASIS FOR
PRAYER MINISTRY

"When Jesus built the church, he built a praying congregation." — **Armin Gesswein**

*I*t's an uncomfortable picture of Jesus. Whip in hand, he overturns the tables of moneychangers and drives out the animals for sacrifice in the temple. All the while, in a loud voice he proclaims the words of the prophets: "Is it not written: 'My house will be called a house of prayer for all nations'? But you have made it 'a den of robbers'" (Mark 11:17).

There is no doubt Jesus came to the temple desiring it to live up to its God-given name, A House of Prayer for all nations. What he found instead was a lot of pseudo-religious activity and no prayer.

Any name is important, regardless of who gives it. There is special significance, though, when God himself steps in to name someone or something. The Bible tells us that God has chosen a name for his own house. In Isaiah 56:7, the Lord says, "These will I bring to my holy mountain and give them joy in my house of prayer. Their burnt offerings and sacrifices will be accepted on my altar; for my house will be called a house of prayer for all nations."

We Are God's House

As we begin to understand that the church today, both corporately and individually, is God's house, it is critical that we comprehend what it means to live in/be a house that has been named by God as a house of prayer. Paul made it clear that we are God's house in Ephesians 2:21-22, "In him (Jesus) the whole building is joined together and rises to become a holy temple in the Lord. And in him you too are being built together to become a dwelling in which God lives by his Spirit."

Paul really emphasized this fact to the Corinthian church.

"Don't you know that you yourselves are God's temple and that God's Spirit dwells in your midst?" (1 Corinthians 3:16).

"Do you not know that your bodies are temples of the Holy Spirit, who is in you, whom you have received from God?" (1 Corinthians 6:19).

"For we are the temple of the living God. As God has said: 'I will live with them and walk among them, and I will be their God, and they will be my people'" (2 Corinthians 6:16).

Peter continues this teaching in 1 Peter 2:5, "You also, like living stones, are being built into a spiritual house to be a holy priesthood." The apostle John records the words of Jesus in Revelation 3:12,"The one who is victorious I will make a pillar in the temple of my God." In the Gospel of John, we hear Jesus say to us: "Anyone who loves me will obey my teaching. My Father will love them, and we will come to them and make our home with them" (John 14:23). Can there be any doubt that the church is the house of God?

We often call Pentecost the birthday of the church. Have you considered the correlation between the events of that day and the day when the first temple was dedicated? As Solomon stood before the people and finished praying his great prayer of dedication, there came from heaven what we often call the Shekinah glory of

God. Fire fell from heaven and consumed the sacrifices and the glory of the presence of the Lord filled the temple. It was clear: God had come to dwell in his house!

On the day of Pentecost as the disciples gathered to pray, God once again dedicated his house. Again, fire fell from heaven. But this time the fire didn't come to a building—it separated and came to rest over the heads of the believers. A new temple was dedicated! And you are that temple. God's house is now his people, both when we are gathered in assemblies as well as individually. What hasn't changed is the name. God's house is still a house of prayer for all nations.

Arms Lifted Up

When a congregation begins to understand that God has named them a house of prayer for all nations, questions begin to arise regarding what prayer is and how we are to pray. One of the most important questions a prayer ministry team must consider is: How does prayer integrate into other ministries happening in a church? To answer, consider the following story from Exodus.

What an old man does with his hands on the top of a mountain shouldn't have any effect on the battle in the valley below. But in the economy of God, it is the work on the mountain that determines the outcome of the battle in the valley. Exodus 17:8-16 gives us the biblical story.

The children of Israel, soon after their exodus from Egyptian slavery, are attacked by the Amalekites. Joshua leads the Israelites in a battle that gives us great insight into the place of prayer. Moses stands on a nearby hill with his hands stretched out to heaven. As long as his arms are lifted, Israel is winning. But when 80-year-old Moses gets tired and lets his arms drop, the battle turns against Israel. Aaron and Hur come to the hill and hold Moses' arms up, and the battle is won.

Arms lifted up is always a picture of prayer. The apostle Paul teaches this in 1 Timothy 2:8, "I want the men everywhere to pray, lifting up holy hands." Israel's victory over the Amalekites is a powerful picture of the place of prayer in the work of the people of God. It was not just prayer that won the victory—Joshua and the army still had to fight. And it certainly wasn't just the fighting, for when prayer stopped, the victory stopped. Our work, with dependence upon God's power in prayer, is the picture of how God wants to advance his kingdom.

> *"Time spent in prayer will yield more than that given to work. Prayer alone gives work its worth and its success. Prayer opens the way for God Himself to do His work in us and through us. Let our chief work as God's messengers be intercession; in it we secure the presence and power of God to go with us."*
> **— Andrew Murray**

It is so easy for a church to lose sight of the critical place of prayer in every aspect of ministry. Yet, when we consider the effort that goes into church work, and often, the meager results, we should realize something is missing. We should be desperate for the power of God to be poured out in our midst as we serve God. Scripture tells us, "You do not have because you do not ask God" (James 4:2), and that is never truer than in the life of a congregation. When prayer is integrated in the life of the people of God, they will begin to see the intervention of Heaven on their behalf and on behalf of others as they minister and serve.

A Critical Foundation

It is this biblical principle that forms the basis for a church prayer ministry. When prayer becomes the foundation for everything that happens in the ministry of a church, God's power is poured out and a whole new level of effectiveness is experienced. Beyond effectiveness in ministry, this biblical process brings increased honor and glory to God and teaches the church to depend fully upon the Lord. Prayer is a key way in which God teaches us to fully trust him.

> *"God's cause is committed to men; God commits Himself to men. Praying men are the vice-regents of God; they do His work and carry out His plans."*
> **— E.M. Bounds**

The purpose of developing a prayer ministry in the local church is twofold: to raise the level of awareness, knowledge, and participation in prayer within the church, and then to seek to advance the kingdom of God by praying individually and corporately for those things on the heart of God as revealed in his Word and through the working of his Spirit.

Paul Billheimer writes in *Destined for the Throne*, "Any church without a well-organized and systematic prayer program is simply operating a religious treadmill." This means prayer must be the cornerstone of every program and activity in the church. We must ask for the Lord's blessing, his presence, and the working of his power—praying for his almighty protection and guidance. Otherwise, we're undertaking ministry in our own strength instead of God's.

A praying church will look much like the church in the New Testament. Perhaps the predominant characteristic of the church in the book of Acts was their prayer life. The church was born on Pentecost, after ten days of continual prayer, and prayer was woven into every aspect of the early church's life. When Luke described the four foundational aspects of church life in Acts 2:42, prayer was one of them. That devotion to prayer expressed in Acts 2 is demonstrated throughout the rest of the book.

When two church leaders were arrested in Jerusalem (Acts 4), the immediate response of the church was to gather and pray. When individuals were needed to take care of distributing food in Jerusalem, the apostles demurred, asserting that they must give themselves to prayer and the ministry of the Word. Peter's escape from prison in Acts 12 comes as a result of the church "earnestly praying to God for him." Barnabas and Saul were sent off on their missionary journeys by the church in Antioch with fasting and prayer (Acts 13). Those instances are just a sampling of the prayer life of these early Christians. Prayer was the lifestyle of the New Testament church. A praying church today is following in their footsteps.

CHAPTER 2

THE WHY OF PRAYER

"History belongs to the intercessors, who believe the future into being." — **Walter Wink**

*I*f we are going to have a sustained movement of prayer, we must have a biblical understanding about the "why" of prayer. Without this understanding, we will default to one of two errors: viewing prayer as simply a way of getting things from God, or seeing it as simply a religious exercise that we are supposed to do. We will never give ourselves to prayer until we see its proper place in the plan of God.

From the beginning, prayer has always been about God, first and foremost. All true prayer originates in the heart of the Father. When the Father wants something done, it is immediately known to the Spirit: "In the same way, no one knows the thoughts of God except the Spirit of God" (1 Corinthians 2:11). Through the Spirit, God's will is made known to the believer. Then, through the name and authority of the Son, we pray back to the Father what he wanted to do in the first place. Mankind has a role—a vital role—but it's all about God! John Wesley said it this way, "All God's works are done in believing prayer."

Again and again, Scripture demonstrates that God has put prayer at a critical junction in how he has chosen to work on planet earth. Prayer is God's way of accomplishing his will in our world.

As we pray his will, we move into that awesome place of privilege where we join with the work of God. It is how we grow spiritually, not just in doing things for God, but also in learning to work with him in complete dependence. Prayer is so important to our spiritual development that it is not an exaggeration to say God will not move until we ask him. Not because he cannot, but he chooses not to so that we might grow in our understanding of his ways and his will.

One of the most significant passages illustrating this is found in the Old Testament book of Ezekiel. The Israelites had continued to reject the word of God given through the prophets, and it was time for the consequences of sin to be felt. Even at that late point, God wanted mercy to triumph over judgment. However, for God's mercy to be poured out, prayer was required. Someone needed to ask him for mercy. God was demonstrating how he had connected his work on earth to the prayers of his people.

"I looked for someone among them who would build up the wall and stand before me in the gap on behalf of the land so I would not have to destroy it, but I found none" (Ezekiel 22:30). If you see a passage of scripture in which the Creator of all things is looking for someone, it is important to pay attention. It certainly signifies something very close to the heart of God.

This rich verse helps us understand the dealings of God with mankind, not just in this situation but throughout time. Unrepentant sin has consequences. In this case, it was the destruction of Jerusalem. But the verse reveals the compassionate heart of the Father, showing that he is even now looking for ways to avoid destroying his people. God has, however, tied his workings to the prayers of his people. So we find the all-powerful Creator looking for an intercessor, someone who would stand in the gap and cry out on behalf of the land so that God might pour out his saving power. None are found, and the city is destroyed.

Our Prayers Make a Difference

This biblical story demonstrates powerfully that our prayers do make a difference. Even God was waiting on someone to pray before he acted. That flies in the face of much of the current belief (unbelief) in prayer that says, "Prayer is important, but after all, God is going to do whatever he wants to do." That was certainly not the case in Ezekiel 22.

There is another excellent illustration of this principle, this time from a positive perspective. In Exodus 32, while Moses is on Mount Sinai receiving the Ten Commandments, the people of Israel turn from true worship and begin to worship a golden calf. God tells Moses he intends to destroy the people. But Moses steps into the gap of intercession and pleads for mercy for his people. God listens, relents, and the nation is saved. Psalm 106:23 refers to that occasion: "So he said he would destroy them, had not Moses, his chosen one, stood in the breach before him to keep his wrath from destroying them." God found someone to stand in the gap (breach), and his mercy triumphed over judgment.

The emphasis on the power and purpose of prayer is clear. God has chosen prayer as his way of accomplishing his will on earth. Jesus taught us to pray this very thing: "Your kingdom come, your will be done, on earth as it is in heaven" (Matthew 6:10). Prayer moves from our preconceived notion that it is a way to get things from God, to the more biblical perspective of prayer as God's tool for bringing about his purposes. We are privileged to be a part of his work on earth through prayer!

With scriptural teaching serving as an anchor, a congregation should move into prayer ministry with the confidence that they are at the center of God's will for the church. The biblical emphasis on prayer should ensure the support of leadership for this ministry. When the ministry of prayer is seen as foundational to the life of the church, it will move from being a side issue to front and center for every aspect of church life.

"When the devil sees a man or woman who really believes in prayer, who knows how to pray, and who really does pray, and, above all, when he sees a whole church on its face before God in prayer, he trembles as much as he ever did, for he knows that his day in that church or community is at an end." — **R.A. Torrey**

It is important at the outset to clarify that the purpose is not just to have a functioning prayer ministry team. The grand, overarching purpose is to have a praying church! It is then that God's power is poured out upon his people and his purposes are accomplished in our lives. Through prayer, God is honored as his people learn to depend upon him in every way.

A Lifestyle of Prayer

With this as our mindset, we realize that prayer ministry is not about events or programs but lifestyles. Though there will be many programmatic elements as prayer is developed and highlighted in the life of the church, it is essential to point beyond the programs to the One addressed in prayer. Individuals will be taught to walk in continual awareness of the presence of the Lord. As this lifestyle is developed individually, prayer becomes a characteristic of the gathered life of the congregation. All that happens in the church can then be undergirded and fueled by powerful prayer.

New Testament Christians were praying Christians. The church was born at a prayer meeting on the day of Pentecost, and the disciples continued to pray as they went on their way proclaiming the good news of Jesus around the world. That really shouldn't surprise us. The leaders of the church, the apostles, had gone to Jesus earlier and asked him to teach them to pray. He did.

Then he instructed them to teach others what he had taught them. From Jesus to the apostles, to the first-century Christians, and down through the years to us, believers have taught and practiced prayer.

CHAPTER 3

THE BIBLICAL EXAMPLE OF A PRAYING CHURCH

"The true church lives and moves and has its being in prayer." — **Leonard Ravenhill**

*A*s we focus on prayer in the book of Acts, we find that it was a core value of the early church. I doubt they used the term "core value" as we often do today, but the Scriptures indicate that prayer had a place in the key priorities of the church. "They devoted themselves to the apostles' teaching and to the fellowship, to the breaking of bread and to prayer" (Acts 2:42). There we find the core values or priorities of the church:

1. Apostles' doctrine
2. Fellowship
3. Breaking of bread
4. Prayer

Is prayer one of the core values of your church? Certainly we all give lip service to its value, but does prayer really find its way into the nuts and bolts of how you "do church"? In all too many congregations, prayer has become only a way of opening and closing meetings or a means of expressing concern for the sick and hurting. In the book of Acts, believers didn't simply say that they were devoted to prayer; they demonstrated it by their actions.

Corporate prayer was a major emphasis in the early church. The disciples understood the importance and power of praying together. From the day of Pentecost, and regularly thereafter, they met for the purpose of prayer:

"They all joined together constantly in prayer"
(Acts 1:14).
"They devoted themselves...to prayer." (Acts 2:42).
"...going up to the temple at the time of prayer..."
(Acts 3:1).
"They raised their voices together in prayer" (Acts 4:24).
"...where many people had gathered and were praying."
(Acts 12:12).
"...after they had fasted and prayed..." (Acts 13:3).
"He knelt down with all of them and prayed."
(Acts 20:36).

If New Testament Christians saw the importance of praying together, shouldn't we? Most would agree it's a good thing for Christians to pray together, but we must move beyond mere intellectual assent and take specific action steps. We must provide good teaching from our pulpits and classrooms concerning the importance and value of corporate prayer. We can offer a wide variety of prayer opportunities for the church, focusing on many needs and topics. We need to be less anxious about the numbers who attend these prayer meetings. A small gathering of three or four people praying can make a real difference.

As we contrast New Testament praying with contemporary praying, it's clear that prayer in the book of Acts was not for outward show. We don't see New Testament Christian leaders coming together to make decisions and opening their discussion with a "word of prayer." Instead, we see Christian leaders coming together who understood that their primary purpose in assembling *was* prayer.

Sometimes out of that prayer time there emerged decisions that would refocus or otherwise impact the entire body of Christ. You see that clearly in the upper room, as the disciples met to pray before Pentecost. Though their purpose was prayer, they stopped the prayer meeting long enough to select a replacement for Judas Iscariot. What a difference from many church "elections" today! Those early Christians would agree with Joy Dawson, who wrote, "Have we become so impressed by the world's systems of strategizing that we fail to avail ourselves of the simple method of waiting on God, listening to His voice, praying out His thoughts, and obeying what the Master Strategist says?"

We see a similar result of prayer in the church at Antioch, where the leaders of the congregation met to fast, pray, and worship. In the midst of their prayers, God initiated an outreach that would take the gospel where it had never been preached before (Acts 13:1-3). That prayer meeting in Antioch released the missionary team of Paul and Barnabas into the world. What impact could our prayer meetings have on reaching the lost?

Praying the Desires of God

Let's take a brief look at another prayer meeting in the book of Acts. Acts 4:24-31 gives us a thorough presentation of the events leading up to the prayer meeting, a transcription of what the disciples prayed, and then a description of the awesome results of their prayer. Peter and John had been arrested for preaching, held in jail, and then ordered by the Sanhedrin never again to speak or teach in the name of Jesus. Upon their release, they returned to the believers and reported the threats made against them. The assembled believers responded by turning the matter over to the Lord in prayer.

They began praying by acknowledging the power of God who created all things. They continued by affirming the truth of Scripture, especially as they saw it being fulfilled in their lives. They quoted the first two verses of Psalm 2 back to God in prayer, and applied those verses to the situation that Jesus faced when spiritual and governmental leaders opposed his ministry. "Why do the nations conspire and the peoples plot in vain? The kings of the earth take their stand and the rulers gather together against the Lord and against his Anointed One." They also recognized the threats they currently faced as part of that same opposition.

Until this point in the prayer, the disciples had asked for nothing. But in Acts 4:29, they asked for boldness from God to continue preaching the good news of Jesus in spite of the authorities' threats. "Now, Lord, consider their threats and enable your servants to speak your word with great boldness."

The disciples used Psalm 2 as a beginning place for their prayer by quoting from it, and then concluded their prayer request by asking God to fulfill that Psalm in their lives. There's more to the second Psalm than the two verses quoted. In this great Messianic Psalm, God the Father speaks to the Son and says, in verse 8, "Ask me, and I will make the nations your inheritance, the ends of the earth your possession." In praying for boldness to continue to speak the Word of God, these early Christians were praying Scripture back to God in a powerful way, asking him to help fulfill that promise to the Son through them. Praying the Word of God is a powerful and effective way to make sure our prayers line up with God's desires.

The result of their prayer? The place where they were meeting was shaken as God showed his pleasure with their request. And that request was answered powerfully. Verse 31 says, "They were all filled with the Holy Spirit and spoke the word of God boldly."

The same God has the same purpose and desire today: that the ends of the earth might hear the good news of Jesus. And when we, the church today, line our prayers up with the heartbeat of God and ask him to grant us boldness to fulfill his purposes, we too will see his power poured out in awesome ways upon the church of Jesus Christ.

CHAPTER 4

PRINCIPLES FOR AN EFFECTIVE
PRAYER MINISTRY

"When prayer has become secondary, or incidental, it has lost its power. Those who are conspicuously men of prayer are those who use prayer as they use food, or air, or light, or money." — **M. E. Andross**

*I*t is clear that God wants every person and every church to be a house of prayer for all nations (Isaiah 56:7; Mark 11:17).

However, we may not be clear about what that looks like individually and corporately. This section will help. Whether you're launching into such a journey with God, or hoping to better understand and experience the prayer ministry journey you've already begun, the ideas here will bring focus and clarity. One thing is very certain: God desires his people to seek his face so he can accomplish his plans and purposes through them!

Although there are numerous ways to develop and sustain prayer ministry in a local church, a prayer ministry team model has proven to be one of the most effective. But simply appointing a prayer ministry team and allowing it to function within its own ministry silo will not result in a transformed church. Here are some key concepts for pastors, church leaders, and prayer ministry team leaders to consider as you shepherd a movement of prayer in the church.

Leadership involvement is vital. The ideal process for the development, growth, and sustainability of a prayer movement in a local church is for pastors and church leaders to first set an example of prayer in their own lives, marriages, families, and ministries. The congregation will see prayer as necessary and important only as they see that their leaders praying and placing great importance on the practice of prayer.

"None but praying leaders can have praying followers."
— E. M. Bounds

Next, leaders should be actively involved in the vision and the process of becoming a praying church. Leaders who are *about* prayer, rather than simply *for* prayer, are crucial to moving forward.

It is essential to be careful about selecting members of the prayer team. These must be people who will prayerfully press into God for his plans and purposes and who are passionate about praying for church leaders and mobilizing the church to pray.

Leaders need to stay closely connected to this team, affirming and supporting them, pushing the prayer movement forward from the pulpit and platform, and continually keeping the vision for becoming a house of prayer for all nations in front of the congregation.

Two elements are paramount: the support and participation of leadership and a clear, God-directed plan to move prayer from the back burner to the full-on strategy for life and ministry. As you step into a prayer-driven future with this in mind, God will move in powerful ways to uniquely establish his kingdom in and through your church.

Take time for discernment. Once church leaders have determined that prayer is foundational to the life and ministry of their congregation, they're faced with this question: "What does a praying church look like here?"

Their answer looks at the context, culture, and community where the prayer ministry team is called to serve. Everyone in leadership and on a prayer ministry team will answer this question differently, although some may have a few similar ideas. Church leaders and the prayer ministry leaders should shape the vision for becoming a praying church by prayerfully discerning together, asking the Lord for his strategy going forward.

> *"Discernment is the listening part of prayer: sitting with a question or decision in God's presence and waiting for the wisdom of God that is given as pure gift."*
> **— Ruth Haley Barton**

Your house of prayer will look very different from other congregations; therefore, it is vital to allow time for a season of coming together and asking the Father to reveal his heart for the kingdom intimacy and work he wants you to step into with him. It is important to be intentionally committed to plan what God wants to bless, rather than ask God to bless whatever you decide to plan.

Discernment that takes place in prayer requires an intense depth of humility, submission, and unity. Only when it becomes clear that God's Spirit is leading, and you are sensing a unity among your team about how to move forward, can you feel confident about taking the next steps. There is no cookie-cutter method for becoming a praying church, but God does have a unique prayer plan for every congregation.

Work carefully to communicate clearly. Evaluate the plan you're discerning with two guidelines. (1) Can your plan be clearly communicated, implemented, and sustained? (2) Are pastoral staff and leaders fully in agreement, engaged, and ready to move forward? When you're certain the answer to both questions is "yes," you're ready to communicate the vision and direction God has given for the prayer movement in your church.

> *"The man who mobilizes the Christian church to pray will make the greatest contribution to world evangelization in history."* — **Andrew Murray**

Leaders need to articulate the vision and passion clearly so that people don't see prayer ministry as just a series of events or programs. Find ways to teach the congregation biblically why prayer will be your foundational strategy for the kingdom work of God. If they don't know why, they won't give themselves to developing a lifestyle of prayer individually, as families, and corporately as the body of Christ.

Recognize that the majority of the congregation struggles in prayer. Congregational buy-in will likely be slower than you would like. Most people have never been trained in prayer and feel very uncomfortable, especially during corporate prayer experiences. Your goal is to help them gain confidence praying in corporate settings, alone, and with their family.

> *"Put need in the center and need becomes the god of our existence. Put God in the center, and God takes care of the needs of our existence."* — **David Chotka**

Encourage people to embrace prayer as a lifestyle. Most adults in your church have grown up in homes where prayer is little practiced or neglected altogether. Many have prayed only during meals or in times of extreme crisis. They have prayed to open and close meetings, have mentioned mostly health issues in their prayer requests, have a distinctive sameness to their prayers, and generally feel inadequate about their prayer lives.

On average, 5 percent of your community of believers are passionate (or what we call "gifted") intercessors. The other 95 percent need help! Even the leaders in most churches struggle with their prayer lives. By now you can recognize this is no easy task; however, prayer is the work God has given to the church! Oswald Chambers said, "Prayer does not fit us for the greater work; prayer is the greater work."

> *"The ultimate purpose of your daily prayer life is not so you can check it off the 'to do' list, but to experience an intimate union with God."* **— One Cry**

The prayer movement should be intergenerational. God has called everyone, young and old, to seek his face and to be intercessors.

"Through the praise of children and infants you have established a stronghold against your enemies, to silence the foe and the avenger" (Psalm 8:2).

"There was also a prophet, Anna, the daughter of Penuel, of the tribe of Asher. She was very old; she had lived with her husband seven years after her marriage, and then was a widow until she was eighty-four. She never left the temple but worshiped night and day, fasting and praying" (Luke 2:36, 37).

God created us for himself and implanted a desire to commune with him in worship and intercession. Families need help raising their kids to be praying people, because most of them have never had such training. The prayer movement in your church must include, encourage, train, and equip the youngest child to the oldest adult to seek the heart of God in relationship and to walk in his ways.

An important thing to consider is that children do not have junior Holy Spirits inside of them. They have all of the fullest potential of God from the very beginning. The elderly are not "done" because they are old. Prayer is the one ministry everyone is called to and can do!

> *"When I was twelve years of age, I felt clearly led to commit myself, in fact, my entire life to the issue of revival, but that began when I was a boy of eight. I was drawn by the Spirit. I can go back right now in my mind and feel something of what I felt as an eight-year-old. Don't tell me that children can't be drawn into the heart of God. I wouldn't waste their lives sending them off into side rooms to listen to idle talk when something significant is going on among the people of God in the sanctuary."*
> **— Richard Owen Roberts**

The prayer movement involves individuals growing stronger in their personal prayer lives, couples learning to pray with one another, families praying together, and a vibrant children's prayer movement. It also involves more corporate expressions of prayer, such as small groups, ministry teams, prayer during corporate worship, and more. All of it takes shape as God leads you to follow his prayer strategy for your unique body of Christ-followers.

Call attention to the work of God in your midst to increase faith. People will be encouraged by answered prayer and seeing God move!

We have lost the art of personal testimony as God works in our midst! Through word of mouth, stories, videos, social media, or print—whatever works—get the word out when God shows up in big or small ways. Encourage people to pay attention to the God who hears and answers prayer!

> *"Faith in a prayer-hearing God will make a prayer-loving Christian."* — **Andrew Murray**

> *"Prayer is the chief exercise of faith."* — **John Calvin**

Stay flexible. The work of the Holy Spirit humbles us and keeps us on our toes! Recognizing that God may call you and others in the congregation to step into the uncomfortable is crucial, but the rewards of obedience are well worth the inconvenience of the unknown or unplanned. You must be willing to be flexible and keep seeking him for the way forward.

Be creative. Everyone has been uniquely created by God to meet with him! We all have different learning styles, personalities, spiritual gifts, and talents. Helping people identify with and practice the variety of ways they feel drawn to communicate with God will change many lives and enliven the prayer movement in the church. Variety in prayer will excite more and more people, and when prayer becomes a delight instead of a duty, your church will take great strides in becoming a house of prayer.

> *"Prayer should not be regarded as a duty which must be performed, but rather as a privilege to be enjoyed, a rare delight that is always revealing some new beauty."*
> — **E. M. Bounds**

Keep the kingdom in mind. The default mode of prayer is usually health issues, a crisis, or our own wants and needs. When people are taught to seek God and strive to know him, they will then be drawn to pray in ways that come alongside of God's plans and purposes. You will see more answered prayer and more people excited to become the answer to the prayers they pray. Most people will need to have their prayer experiences stretched outside of their comfort zones to embrace what is on the heart of God.

> *"Our ordinary views of prayer are not found in the New Testament. We look upon prayer as a means for getting something for ourselves; the Bible idea of prayer is that we may get to know God Himself."*
> **— Oswald Chambers**

Lost people, unity in the body, those in authority, workers for the harvest field—all these are important to the Father, but are not in the normal, everyday mindset of people as they pray. Scripture is the best teacher for knowing the will and heart of God as we intercede. When God tells us to pray about certain things, he means for us obediently to do so; however, this will take teaching, training, and practice! Every prayer should bring glory to the Father. When everyone in the congregation recognizes this, their prayer lives will be different.

Prayer is central to worship. "Worship is at the heart of what the church is and does," says Alvin Vander Griend. "It is the defining event that sets the tone for all of the church's life. The success or failure of a congregation's ministry will depend on its worship. And prayer is at the very heart of worship. It's a two-way communication by which love flows between God and God's people. Let's make every effort to claim all that God intended for us in prayer—the chief means by which to maintain and grow our relationship with God and to partner with God in winning a lost world."

When we focus our attention on God it is worship, whether we are singing our prayers or speaking them. God is worthy of our worship, and he delights in our expressions of praise focused upon him. By calling attention to the One who is on the other end of our prayers, people will grow in their relationship with him. Engaging the worship team in teaching prayer will be a key component for a praying church.

Make space for prayer. In most churches, creating space for prayer is often difficult. If you haven't already done so, your prayer ministry needs a dedicated prayer room that is not used for other purposes such as storage, counseling, classes, or other meetings. If finding such a space is difficult, pray about it. Ask pastoral staff, intercessory teams, and other church leaders to join you. Usually some kind of solution can be found, and it is vital to do so.

> *"Let the fires go out in the boiler room of the church and the place will still look smart and clean, but it will be cold. The Prayer Room is the boiler room for its spiritual life."*
> **— Leonard Ravenhill**

But remember that just having a prayer room is not an end in itself. If no one ever uses it, there is no reason to have it. Your prayer room should be dedicated to the practice of prayer, so its furnishings and finishes should reflect the activity of prayer. A beautifully decorated room does not a war room make!

Make time for prayer. Looking at a church calendar can give much insight into what a congregation believes is important. The presence on the calendar of prayer activity should begin to increase as the prayer movement of the church gains traction. R.A. Torrey's observation should motivate us. "We are too busy to pray, and so we are too busy to have power. We have a great deal of activity, but we accomplish little; many services but few conversions; much machinery but few results."

Develop a budget. What price tag should be placed on prayer becoming the foundational strategy of your congregation's life and ministry? What will it take to become known as a praying church in your community?

> *"When the Church sets itself to pray with the same seriousness and strength of purpose that it has devoted to other forms of Christian effort, it will see the Kingdom of God come with power."*
> **— Report of The Edinburgh Missionary Conference**

For leaders, giving value to the prayer ministry means finding a way to fund the process of developing and sustaining a movement of prayer. This may include setting up the prayer room, training the prayer team members and intercessors, creating a variety of prayer experiences for the congregation, and collecting materials and resources. Some churches consider additional technology for their prayer ministry, such as purchasing a satellite dish to broadcast national prayer events in their sanctuaries. This can bless not only your own congregation, but also others around you.

Prayer ministry teams should be very meticulous about creating a proposed budget, whether in your first year of existence or well along in the process of becoming a praying church. Present your budget in a professional way, allowing someone gifted in this area to take the lead.

It is much easier to establish a budget with someone from the pastoral staff and/or leadership team involved in the process.

Support and acknowledge the prayer ministry team. If any team needs the guidance and participation of the leadership, this team does. They can facilitate prayer in such a way that it will impact every single ministry in the life of your church family! But they will need the help and accountability of leaders.

Supporting, and even commissioning, the prayer ministry team is important so the congregation is aware that becoming a praying church is a high priority for the pastor(s) and leaders. They need to know that the people who will foster this movement of prayer, along with the leaders, have the full support of these leaders. Consider commissioning your prayer team during a worship service, and have the congregation surround them in prayer. The enemy will stop at nothing to halt the prayer movement in your church. They need to have others praying for them!

SECTION 2

PRAYER MINISTRY TEAM

*W*hile prayer ministry in the local church may be led by the senior pastor or someone on the pastoral staff, it is often led by a volunteer, a layperson with a heart for prayer. Recognizing this, the content in this section is designed to help equip both the prayer team leader, and the prayer team members.

CHAPTER 5

FOR THE PRAYER TEAM MEMBERS

"Discipleship does not mean to use God when we can no longer function ourselves. On the contrary, it means to recognize that we can do nothing at all, but that God can do everything through us. As disciples, we find not some but all of our strength, hope, courage, and confidence in God. Therefore, prayer must be our first concern."
— Henri Nouwen

The Team

The primary function of an effective prayer ministry team should be to uphold the leaders of the church in constant prayer, teaching and training others to do the same.

The team should prayerfully, patiently, and consistently motivate and call the congregation to pray. The team is responsible for training and equipping people of all ages through teaching and providing multiple opportunities and resources. Essentially, the prayer ministry team members are the *prayer mobilizers* for the church.

Team members are passionate about individual and corporate prayer, but that's not all. They are the planners, organizers, and creative visionaries for what God wants to accomplish through prayer in the life of the church. Always, the call of Jesus to be a house of prayer for all nations is before us.

Functioning Together

Once the team starts taking shape, the first order of business is to spend time together before the Lord in prayer, seeking God's direction. Be sure the prayer ministry is built on the foundation of prayer and guided by the leading of the Holy Spirit. It should not be just another man-made program.

> *"It's the people who 'ride the high places' with God who, in partnership with Him, determine the affairs of humankind living in the valleys and plains below."* — **Jack Hayford**

There are so many potential opportunities and exciting prayer events that it is very easy to fall into a trap that will slow down God's plans if you are not carefully seeking him first. This snare is set by the enemy to confuse, overwhelm, discourage, and cause dissension among team members and the leadership of the church.

Once you are united together for the purpose of encouraging the church to pray, be certain to focus on God's desires for the church instead of your own. Remember, do not be deceived by the temptation to ask God to bless what you are planning. Instead, plan those things God wishes to bless.

Roles and Functions

The following is simply intended to get you thinking about areas of involvement and skill sets you might need to give you a well-rounded prayer ministry team. Do remember that God is perfectly capable of gifting whoever is on the team for these tasks, so don't be concerned with finding "just the right people." God will guide, direct, provide, and faithfully respond to your every need as you align yourselves with his prayer movement.

Please remember that this team should be intergenerational, so don't discount the gifts of younger people as well as seniors. Just as Paul mentored Timothy, you should find and encourage young people who are passionate about prayer or interested in learning more about prayer. Meanwhile, some seniors might be or could become the most fervent intercessors in your congregation. And many seniors, afraid that their days of usefulness are over, would welcome the gift of joining your prayer team.

Prayerfully ask the Father to bring the right people to your team or to help you locate them. Because every church is different, you may find that not all of the areas listed below are a necessity. You may also find that God leads you to different kinds of people— who all fit into whatever plan he has shown you for your church. Also, remember that there will be people on the prayer ministry team who can take on multiple roles.

Ask God to lead you and your coordinator to those with the gifts your team needs most. Decide which of the roles and functions in the list below can be filled by the members already on your team. This would be a good discussion for a team meeting. Sometimes one person can see the gifts in another person better than they can see them in themselves.

The administratively gifted. These people can pull together a plan from start to finish and keep everything organized. They are able to delegate, keep people on task to meet deadlines, and create and monitor the budget.

The creative. They can take an idea or plan and find creative ways to give it life. They not only think creatively but also can bring together what is needed to implement the idea. For example, if a season of prayer is being planned, they are the ones to develop prayer stations or short segments of prayer that will engage people of all ages and with a variety of temperaments and personalities. Creatives can take ideas and bring them to life in a variety of expressive ways to lead people into the presence of God.

The servants. These team members will do whatever is asked of them. If there is a need to set up a room in a certain way or to help the creative people with their work, these people humbly make themselves available. Often, they just want to be told what is needed, and they will be off and running with a willing heart.

"If prayer leads us into a deeper unity with the compassionate Christ, it will always give rise to concrete acts of service." — **Henri Nouwen**

The communicators. These team members "get the word out" to the congregation via every means possible: print, social media, text messaging, web, and more. They develop and create short videos, flyers, bulletin inserts, or any other piece that will help involve, train, motivate, or encourage people to pray.

The scheduler. He or she keeps in touch with whoever schedules rooms and keeps the church calendar. If your church has teams of people praying regularly for different activities (for example, during or before worship services), the scheduler makes sure someone is assigned to each one. This is the person who connects with other ministries to set up training. For example, if prayer is going to be infused into the church's small group ministry, the scheduler sets up a meeting with the small group leaders. Much of this will be decided upon during team meetings.

The utility player. This team member fits into multiple categories and can be called into service or jump into unfilled spots as needed.

The intercessors. They are the team's prayer warriors. They pray for the team, the church leaders, and the congregation. They pray for the church to become a praying church, glorifying God and serving Christ's kingdom purposes!

PRAYER MINISTRY VOLUNTEER HANDBOOK

> *"History belongs to the intercessors, who believe the future into being. If this is so, then intercession, far from being an escape from action, is a means of focusing for action and of creating action. By means of our intercessions, we veritably cast fire upon the earth and trumpet the future into being."* — **Walter Wink**

They also connect with other praying people to keep them informed. For example, if on Sundays there is some kind of card people use to make prayer requests, the intercessors will collect, compile, and distribute them to the pastors, staff, other leaders, and intercessors recruited to pray for such requests.

They may also follow up to see how God is answering and report answered prayers and updates. It is important for the congregation to hear how the Father is answering the prayers of his people! This encourages and builds faith.

> *"The church that is not jealously protected by mighty intercession and sacrificial labors will before long become the abode of every evil bird and the hiding place for unsuspected corruption. The creeping wilderness will soon take over that church that trusts in its own strength and forgets to watch and pray."* — **A.W. Tozer**

The teacher/trainer/mentor. It is important to have one or more people on the prayer ministry team who can teach, train, and mentor in prayer, or who works with those who will be doing such teaching. If a prayer seminar, prayer weekend, or prayer emphasis needs teaching, this person will take the lead

The liaisons. They translate the prayer ministry for other ministry team leaders in the church. They communicate and facilitate the vision of prayer as the primary strategy for the kingdom purposes of God in every aspect of church life.

Liaisons are good communicators, filled with grace, and able to work with leaders in each area of church ministry.

Liaisons are also needed to connect with prayer ministries in other churches in your community. If your church wishes to be a light bearer to the community and a place that fosters unity, it begins in prayer. Reaching out to other churches, inviting them to join you in prayer or a prayer event, such as the National Day of Prayer, allows you to take steps closer to the purposes and plans of God for your community.

Recruiter/trainer. This team member will help where it is important to recruit and train people who may not be formally on the prayer ministry team, but who are a vital part of the church's prayer ministry. For example, your church might decide to have teams up front to pray with those who come forward for prayer during the service. If so, these people will need to be recruited and trained.

(Find the personal qualifications for Prayer Team members in Chapter 9.)

Doing the Work of Prayer Ministry

Identify and evaluate existing prayer efforts. It is important to evaluate what the church is already doing in the area of prayer. Is there an existing prayer chain? A men's prayer breakfast? A group that meets regularly to pray for the pastors?

After you have assessed the prayer happening in the church currently, your job is not to do away with these initiatives in favor of new ones; rather, it is to prayerfully evaluate the effectiveness of the existing ministries and, if possible, to incorporate them into a unified ministry of prayer. If you find, for example, that your prayer chain has become a gossip chain and is a hindrance to the church instead of a vital ministry, some teaching and reorganization may be in order before beginning again with fresh vision.

Seek wisdom before you seek change (Proverbs 24:3; James 1:5).

Move forward ONLY as God leads and the Holy Spirit guides. Be careful not to succumb to the most dangerous temptation when beginning a prayer ministry: doing too much too quickly. Always remember that the prayer ministry is a servant-driven ministry, functioning in complete obedience to the leading of the Holy Spirit and under the authority of church leadership.

Beware of the enemy's attempts to discourage you. For example, don't feel bad if there's poor turnout at prayer gatherings, and don't succumb to the temptation to make others, especially leaders, feel guilty for not participating. God will draw people into *his* prayer movement, not yours.

> *"Prayer warriors are the most frightening, powerful, demon-chasing, world-moving beings on earth...prayer warriors are positioned by God to stand in faith for their families and churches and cities. Prayer is stronger than kings and mightier than armies. Prayer is the most powerful force on earth."*
> **— Francis Frangipane**

Your team is the vessel God can use to draw his people into an intimate relationship with him. Many people will respond to urgent or immediate needs in prayer. Others will resonate with a specific purpose, such as coming together to pray for schools, for the nation, for missionaries, or for the sick. And some will get excited about participating in a special prayer experience. God places certain burdens on the hearts of his people, whether they are clearly aware of it or not.

Everyone in your church will not be a seasoned intercessor. In fact, many are unaware that prayer is much more than a religious thing that Christians are supposed to do, rather than a relationship with the living God. With solid teaching and experience, your church can become the house of prayer God desires it to be.

Determine what resources already exist and can be made available to the team and to the congregation. Are there books, videos, classes, prayer groups, devotionals, mentoring or discipleship opportunities, or seminars accessible for learning and growth? If not, consider obtaining resources—as God provides the means—through your budget. If you don't have a budget, consider talking to the church leader who gives oversight to the prayer ministry.

You may choose to incorporate these resources into your church library, or establish a separate library or resource center near or adjacent to your prayer room. Don't forget the abundance of online resources available and easily accessible. (See also Chapter 24: Resources for Further Help and Study.)

Give everyone an opportunity to plug into God's prayer movement in your church. Schedule prayer experiences at different times and for different purposes. Each prayer time should have a specific focus and direction. The surroundings should always be conducive to prayer (maps of the world, pictures of missionary families and church members, etc.). When people come to pray, they need to have a positive experience and leave feeling their prayers have been heard. Preparing a space and time for the people of God to meet with God is a huge responsibility. There are many examples to help you in Section 3.

Keep prayer fresh, exciting, and vital. Change things up consistently so that there is always something different. Perhaps a prayer walk one time and using prayer stations the next. Giving people opportunities to participate in exciting, refreshing times of prayer different from the "way it has always been" is very important. You will have many good suggestions in Section 3.

Be sure to talk with your pastor about allowing time for testimonies of answered prayer during church services. Our faith grows when we hear how powerfully God works in answer to our prayers, whether in our midst or in the lives of those who live thousands of miles away.

Be sure God is always the honored guest and his glory is always the focus in prayer. God should always receive all of the glory, honor, and praise as he works in our lives and in the lives of others. Be sensitive to the leading of his Spirit as you make plans for incorporating prayer into the life of the church. Find out what God wants to accomplish and join him.

Come alongside other ministries to help prayer become their strategy for greater kingdom effectiveness. Work with ministry leaders to cast vision and share ideas for how prayer can be integrated into all plans, activities, events, and meetings.

Remember: the devil hates prayer. The enemy hates prayer and will do anything he can to discourage, dissuade, damage, and destroy your team's unity, reputation, and forward progress. He will likely try to damage you, your marriages, your children, and your ministries. Be prepared and stay alert! Put on the armor of God daily to protect yourselves from the attacks the enemy will throw at you. Be sure intercessors are covering you all continually!

"Satan trembles when he sees, the weakest saint upon his knees." — **William Cowper**

One step at a time! Your progress may be small at first, so don't be discouraged that huge changes aren't taking place in the beginning. Don't let the enemy of our souls discourage you when a handful of people show up to prayer gatherings. People come into the prayer movement as the Spirit draws them, and as they deepen their relationship with Jesus through communing with him in the fellowship of prayer. The prayer ministry team facilitates this relationship and creates space and opportunity for people to learn how to approach the throne of grace with boldness (Hebrews 4:16) and to show them how continually to live in the throne room of heaven.

John Quam's insight underlines this point. "No church can begin every kind of prayer initiative at once," he wrote. "Beginning with a few key strategies will help pave the way for other types of prayer. The process for reevaluating the priorities and deciding what's next is an ongoing one. Mapping out a long-term vision is always helpful as long as we hold it lightly and allow God to take us in a different direction if He should so choose."

CHAPTER 6

FOR THE PRAYER TEAM LEADER/ COORDINATOR

"The presence of God in the midst of a church is directly proportional to the amount of prayer that takes place there." — **Dr. Tommy Barnett**

A structure of support, involvement, communication, and accountability between the prayer ministry team leader and other church leaders is vital to fulfilling the mandate of Jesus to become a house of prayer for all nations.

Maybe you are the person filling this role at your church. Or maybe your team is forming, but a leader has not been designated. In that case, ask God to raise up his choice for the leader. The team leader may or may not be the "best pray-er" in the congregation. It is more important that he or she combine their passion for prayer with administrative gifts and people skills.

Occasionally, we find a prayer ministry team led by someone who is gifted both in intercession and administration. It is very rare, but is truly ideal! The team leader must be able to see the prayer needs of the congregation and get a vision for what a praying church should look like. It is truly a gift if this person also regularly spends hours in prayer!

Role and Function

Vision. The prayer team leader carries an extremely important mantle as he/she prayerfully keeps God's directive to become a house of prayer for all nations in the forefront of every action. Seeking God for each step will keep the coordinator following God's agenda rather than their own. The prayer team leader is the key mobilizer for the ministry of prayer, as established by church leaders' discernment of God's plan to become a praying church.

Accountability. The team leader is accountable to whatever staff or leadership person has been designated to function as the overseer of the prayer ministry for the congregation and stays in close communication with that person. Being the liaison between leadership and the prayer ministry team is very important.

Intercession. The prayer team leader regularly prays for the pastoral staff and leaders, the team members, and the congregation. He or she should also pray over the vision and direction God has given for how the church is to become a house of prayer for all nations.

Recruitment. The prayer team leader is involved in the recruiting and selection of other prayer ministry team members. It is most important to ask God to send or make known the people he has in mind for the team. Their hearts are more important than their identified gifts. Ask the Father to bring just the right skill sets to help you guide the congregation in the ministry of prayer. As you find gaps, you can be more specific about the people who are needed to round out the prayer team.

What is the best way to find them and recruit them? Perhaps the best advice is to follow the example of Jesus before he chose the twelve apostles. "Jesus went out to a mountainside to pray, and spent the night praying to God" (Luke 6:12).

After a night of prayer, he chose the twelve from among his disciples. It was not a task that was undertaken lightly. He didn't just say, "Who wants to be an apostle?" and then take the first twelve to volunteer. We can only assume that he prayerfully asked God to help him make wise choices. In the same way, the team leader and church leaders should prayerfully seek men, women, and young people God seems to be setting apart for this ministry.

Organization. The team leader establishes the structure of the team and identifies roles for team members. This process can take some time and will require good discernment skills on the part of the team leader. Sometimes it takes a while to determine who best fits into what role(s).

Oversight and delegation. The effective team leader is careful not to micromanage the team. After choosing competent people, the leader trusts them to minister with full accountability to the team leader and the church leadership. The team members need space to hear from God and mobilize prayer.

The leader's encouragement and support are very important—sometimes that means allowing this team to stumble a bit as they learn and grow. The leader celebrates with them and is careful about giving unsought suggestions or guidance. If team members don't feel they have the leader's blessing, this prayer movement will not be sustainable.

Support. The team leader is a servant, prayer warrior, and encourager to pastors, leaders, and team members.

A team leader leads by example and should always be willing to encourage and help whenever it is needed. He or she should regularly ask the pastoral and leadership teams how they want to be prayed for and share those requests with team members. Let the leaders in the church know that the prayer ministry team always has their backs in prayer. This will be of tremendous encouragement.

If the devil wants to take down a church, he will do it by taking down leaders. Praying for them and building teams to pray for them is crucial! If the congregation is continually praying for their leaders, they won't be griping and complaining to or about them.

(Find the personal qualifications for the Prayer Ministry Team Leader in Chapter 9.)

Identify and Recruit Team Members

A dynamic prayer ministry is always on the lookout for new team members. God can use every member of the team as the spiritual eyes and ears to consider the makeup of a prayer ministry team. The first step, and an ongoing matter for prayer, is "God, lead us to the right combination of workers to achieve your purposes here."

After that, asking some key questions will help identify those the Lord may have placed in plain sight. For example, who shows up regularly at prayer meetings or events? Who is willing to lead out in prayer? Who has a consistent personal prayer life? When a class or seminar on prayer is offered, who is there? What about the person who has a consistent burden to pray for missionaries or pastors or those who are sick?

Sometimes we may overlook people who are not always obvious to us. Many people who deeply desire to see the church become a house of prayer for all nations aren't advertising that fact, but they ARE praying about it! Ask God to connect you with them.

Remember that many of these people will not just volunteer for prayer ministry unless they are invited or obviously called by God to such ministry. Never assume someone wouldn't be interested or that they are too busy. Be intentional about asking them to help when you have identified someone who has the gifts you need to be on the team.

Errors to Avoid

How is your prayer ministry team currently functioning? If you sense that it could be more effective, take time to pray about who is currently serving on your team. Make sure you're not suffering from the effects of two misguided, but understandable, errors.

The 5 percent error. Scripture tells us in multiple places that we are all to intercede. But we know that gifted intercessors—those who are called to deeper levels of intercession—make up only 5 percent of the congregation, usually. These are the folks whose deepest desire is to spend time before the Lord in prayer and fasting. They are your "Annas and Simeons." They may already meet together in prayer, but they also spend much time in private prayer. They can stay in one room for several hours at a time, praying earnestly. They are known as the "go-to" people when prayer is needed.

What happens when these "gifted intercessors" are chosen to be the prayer ministry team? Too often leaders remove them from their primary area of giftedness, intercession, and place them into an administrative role they are not usually equipped or called to do.

If the prayer ministry team is made up completely of gifted intercessors, they will plan prayer meetings, events, and experiences for others who pray like they do, because that is all they know. The majority of the congregation, if they are even motivated to attend, will likely feel intimidated, bored, or frustrated with such gatherings.

But sometimes, instead of seeking out the intercessors, pastors or other leaders immediately reject them. This happens when the pastor has had a bad experience with one or more of them. They may have heard, "The Lord told me to tell you..." one too many times. Or the intercessors have been critical because their pastor/

leaders do not seem to have the same passion for prayer they do. Rather than praying for the spiritual lives of their leaders, they criticize and grumble to others.

It is very important that pastors and intercessors have a healthy, strong relationship built on mutual respect. This takes time and effort on both sides, and sometimes requires some mediation so that the prayer movement can move forward.

With all of that said, it is important to have at least one gifted intercessor on your prayer ministry team. The size of the congregation and the needs of the team may suggest recruiting more than one. These intercessors will continually call the visionaries and planners back to the heart of the Father.

The silo error. The second common error is to make the prayer ministry just one more activity or program in the church.

Just having a prayer ministry team doesn't mean much unless there is a clear vision of the calling to become a house of prayer for all nations—a praying church! This means prayer is infused into every ministry, every event, and every outreach so that God's Spirit is free to move at will throughout the life and work of the church. If the prayer ministry team remains marginalized, separated, or siloed, it will not have the chance to saturate the lives of all the people and all the ministries of the church.

SECTION 3

PRAYER MINISTRY TOOLS

*T*hink of this section as your prayer ministry tool kit. Here is where you will find a multitude of practical ideas, tips, and helps. From multiple approaches to prayer, to prayer meeting outlines, and much more, these tried and tested tools will help you build a viable and sustainable house of prayer.

CHAPTER 7

IMPORTANT REMINDERS

"Prayer is not a program. It's a movement beginning in the heart of God. Still, your prayer ministry will benefit from structure because 'God is not a God of disorder but of peace' (1 Corinthians 14:33)."
— Onie Kittle

- As you peruse this resource section, it will be very easy to get excited about all of the possibilities of prayer and lose sight of the main thing: becoming a house of prayer for all nations (a praying church).
- A praying church fosters a foundational, sustainable lifestyle strategy of prayer that fuels every ministry, event, and mission of the church for the sake of God's glory!
- A praying church allows the Holy Spirit to guide the process of discerning what the house of prayer at your church will look like and be known as. Be sure you have pursued His perfect plan through a season of discernment with your team and church leadership.
- Your church's house of prayer will make a significant kingdom impact!

CHAPTER 8

EIGHT BASIC APPROACHES
TO PRAYER

*H*ere are some easy-to-teach beginning places for those who are learning how to pray. They are especially good for children, but any adult can relate to them as well. Acronyms are helpful teaching tools for many people.

ACTS

ADORATION – Give God praise and honor for who he is as Lord over all.

CONFESSION – Deal with the sin in your life, repent of it, and ask God's forgiveness.

THANKSGIVING –Tell God all you are grateful for in your life.

SUPPLICATION – Pray for the needs of others and yourself.

PRAY

PRAISE – Focus on God's amazing attributes.

REPENT – Recognize our sinfulness, confessing it to God and repenting of it.

ASK – Consider first what is on the heart of God and pray his plans and purposes; next, make your own requests of God.

YIELD – Pray, "Not my will but Yours be done!" Yield to the purposes of God.

BLESS

A simple way to pray for family, friends, neighbors, and missionaries is by using the acronym BLESS. Pray five blessings for five people for five minutes a day for five days a week for five weeks:

BODY – Health, safety and physical needs

LABOR – Someone's work or school situation

EMOTIONAL NEEDS – The emotional needs of others – for joy, peace and hope

SOCIAL NEEDS – Relationships: friendships, marriages, families

SPIRITUAL NEEDS – Salvation, grace, and faith

THUMB PRAYER

TRIBAL – Usually animists who believe in spirits that live around us, in trees, rocks, etc. They live their lives in fear trying to keep these spirits happy.

HINDU – Believe in thousands of gods; the Christian God might be just one of these, rather than the only true God. They believe in reincarnation, coming back to life in another form after death.

UNRELIGIOUS – The largest group of unreached people is a conglomeration of many beliefs. The largest number are in China. However, they can also be nominal Christians who say they believe but are disconnected from church and haven't actively engaged Jesus as Savior and Lord.

MUSLIM – Believe in one god but not one they can address as "father." Jesus was a prophet but not God, and was not crucified for our sins.

BUDDHIST – Believe in following a path of discipline to reach a state of enlightenment. Usually there is no connection to a god at all.

ORPHANS – Children like to add this one to pray for other children; have them pray for the children in the THUMB also!

Pray for:
- ° Opportunities to hear about God and His plan for salvation.
- ° Understanding of sin and a desire for a Savior.
- ° Entire families and communities to love Jesus as Lord and Savior.
- ° Courage and protection for new believers so that they can share the Good News.

It's good to help people understand what these other religions believe and specific ways to pray for each.

PRAISE

PRAISE (Psalm 100:4)
REPENTANCE (1 John 1:9; 2 Corinthians 7:10)
ASK (Luke 11:9)
INTERCEDE (Hebrews 7:25)
SPEAK THE WORD (Mark 11:21-24; Matthew 4:1-4)
ENJOY (Psalm 16:11)

ONE WORD PRAYERS

WOW (praise)
OOPS (confession)
THANKS (thanksgiving)
PLEASE (intercession and supplication)

"If thanks was the only prayer we ever said, we would be very holy people." — **Meister Eckhart**

FIVE FINGERS
Pray Each Day for 5 Days

Two ways to use 5 fingers to pray
Option 1:
Thumb: Praise God
Index Finger: Confession
Middle Finger: Thanksgiving
Ring Finger: Intercession
Pinkie: Petition

Option 2:
Thumb: Family and Friends
Index Finger: Teachers/Co-workers/neighbors
Middle Finger: Church Leaders
Ring Finger: Sick/poor
Pinkie: Self

PRAY NOW!
When we are asked to pray for someone, we usually say we will but either forget, or wait for a while until we think of this person or need again. Train people to stop and pray right then instead of waiting. It will bless the person who asked for prayer and will allow the person praying to fulfill the assignment promptly! It doesn't have to be a long, detailed prayer, just a simple ask to the One who holds the past, present, and future in his hands.

CHAPTER 9

PRAYER MINISTRY TEAM QUALIFICATIONS

Qualifications for a Prayer Ministry Team Leader

*G*od has named every church a house of prayer for all nations. What that looks like is different for every church. Selecting a person to lead the prayer ministry of your church, under the authority of and alongside the vision God has set before leaders, is critically important. The prayer ministry team leader may be a volunteer or on staff. Here is a sample list of qualifications to consider when making such a choice. But always remember, it is most important to seek the person God wishes to raise up.

A prayer ministry team leader...

- Is a believer in Jesus Christ, as demonstrated by consistently striving for personal holiness and a deeper relationship with the Lord through prayer and service.
- Senses a strong call from the Lord to be a leader in the area of prayer, confirmed by leaders in the church and other spiritual advisors.
- Is respected and trusted by the leadership and members of the church, and recognized as one who is spiritually mature.
- Has enough time to devote to the ministry.
- Desires to foster unity in prayer within the church and community.

- Recognizes the need for nurturing and discipling others in individual, family, and corporate prayer.
- Has gifts to organize, encourage, and give leadership in prayer, as evidenced by demonstrated gifts of administration, communication, and leadership.
- Will seek the Lord for what he desires the prayer ministry team to be, and has the ability to delegate tasks to team members according to their gifts and abilities.
- Will freely submit to the authority of God and the church leadership.
- Functions from a position of humility rather than seeking recognition.
- Brings out the best in others and does not micromanage.
- Is able to quell grumbling and criticism on the ministry team with love and prayer and is not personally critical in any way of church leadership or church members.
- Recognizes the importance of a team and understands that one person cannot build and sustain a prayer movement in a church!
- Makes sure pastors, leaders, the congregation, and team members are prayed for.
- Understands the prayer team can make plans, but it is God's strategy. Is willing to take step at a time. "Many are the plans in a person's heart, but it is the Lord's purpose that prevails" (Proverbs 19:21).

Qualifications for a Prayer Ministry Team Member

- Is a believer in Jesus Christ as demonstrated by consistently striving for personal holiness and a deeper relationship with the Lord through prayer and service.

- Has a heart for prayer and a passion for the lost.
- Desires to help people learn to pray better and more effectively.
- Desires to help the church come together to pray (as in the example of the early church throughout the book of Acts).
- Has gifts and abilities consistent with the needs of the prayer team for calling the church to prayer and helping to integrate prayer into every aspect of church life and ministry.
- Has faith to believe in the power of prayer to change lives and circumstances.
- Is willing to pray earnestly and continually for pastoral staff and church leadership, for the prayer team leader, and for the congregation.
- With a servant's heart, is willing to serve and use his or her gifts and talents under the leadership and accountability of the prayer team coordinator.
- Has time to devote to the team and the tasks he or she will undertake, and is able to meet deadlines as necessary.

CHAPTER 10

PRAYER BEFORE AND DURING THE WORSHIP SERVICE

*H*ere are some ways to integrate prayer before, during, and after your worship services and other events so that every time someone enters or leaves your church, they have an opportunity to encounter God in prayer. Covering your campus with prayer can be a powerful way to begin or elevate the prayer movement. This has a special impact on visitors who will see that yours is a praying church.

Before the Service

Each week a team of intercessors can pray as they walk around and through the building. Here are some examples.

- **Walk around the outside of the building,** asking for God's protection against anything the enemy may be planning to do to disrupt or damage people, pastors and leaders, teachers, technicians, equipment, etc.

- If your church uses **parking attendants,** train them to pray for those coming onto the church grounds. Even if you don't routinely use people to help with parking, train and assign some people to pay attention and intercede as people are driving onto the church property.

- **Give these team members training.** Provide a list of Scriptures and blessings they can pray for people as they drive onto the property. Some come with problems. Some have struggled to get the whole family ready on time. Anticipate the needs of those arriving.

  For example, if people look sad, pray for the joy of the Lord to invade their hearts. If a family is arriving at church together, pray for God to give them peace and great love for one another. If a person is alone, ask God to help them feel welcomed and that they would be surrounded by fellowship and God's love through every interaction with others. Use the BLESS prayer (Chapter 8), or the list of blessings in the praying Scripture part of Chapter 14.

Prayer Walking the Building

Intercessors walk through every part of the building, praying for every aspect of what will take place before, during, and after the worship service.

- **Sanctuary.** Assign different sections to different intercessors who touch each seat or row, asking God to move in the heart of the person(s) who will sit there.
- **Technology and instruments.** Intercessors go to the stage and the sound booth to pray for everything to function as it should and that each person operating the equipment would be alert and aware, excelling in their work for the Lord in these areas. Cover the instruments in prayer as well.
- **Green room or wherever the pastors and worship team gather before worship.** Pray for God to

pour out unity and giftedness for the purpose of leading people to the throne of grace.

- **Children and youth areas**. Walk through each classroom and space used by the children and youth, asking God to touch the hearts and minds of these younger generations so that they might be on fire for Jesus Christ. Pray for their leaders and teachers to be on time, prepared, and empowered by the Spirit to lead these young ones. Pray for their worship times, technology, etc. as well.

Prayer Room

In preparation for each worship service, intercessors should pray for every aspect of the service ahead of time. They should be available to pray for the preacher, worship team, technicians, and anyone involved in the service who has an opportunity to come in for prayer.

Floating Prayer Teams

If your church has a space where people can gather before and after services, it's a great idea to train teams of people to wander the area making themselves available to pray with people. They should wear a sign or button that says something like, "Need Prayer?" It is surprising how many will take you up on getting some much needed prayer before or after the service. As people begin to see others praying in the common areas, prayer will become more common as others pray for one another spontaneously.

What if the floating prayer team discovers an issue that needs follow-up? Take the person to the prayer room for more in-depth prayer, or be sure they know the people to connect with for more resources. Prepare those who do counseling, whether marital, financial, or other, to be ready to help set up an appointment or make a referral for those who have need. Have a pager or text system set up so such counselors can be notified when they are needed.

During Worship Services

Altar Prayer Teams

Purpose: to provide prayer support for the congregation during worship services.

Sometimes people are moved in response to God during the worship service or after the message. Without a place to seek him either alone or with others, this moment of need or conviction may pass. Something significant happens when a church creates space for people to respond to the Holy Spirit's urging in addition to responses during the typical invitation hymn.

Some come into worship services damaged, disappointed, disillusioned, uncertain, or guilt-ridden, and they need something significant to happen in their hungry souls. When the Spirit moves in their hearts during the service and there is no place to seek God or to express their burden, the moment may pass. And then people leave unchanged, because there was no opportunity to experience the love and power of God that prayer can offer.

Structure of a team: Two men, two women, or a married couple. Two people of the opposite sex who are not married should not be on a team together (unless it is a team of three or more). Also consider training young people to be part of the altar prayer teams.

The number of teams should be determined by the size of the congregation and the expected need. (If the pastor is preaching on a particularly sensitive subject, he may alert the prayer ministry team coordinator to add extra teams.) There should also be teams on call who are watchful during the season of prayer and can step in if all other teams are occupied and praying for people. There should be no people standing in line to be prayed for. Waiting may prompt them to decide not to ask for prayer.

Every team should be trained in a similar way (see Chapter 11: Intercessory Prayer Teams).

The main focus for the prayer team is simply to ask those who come for prayer, "How can I pray for you?" It is important not to move into a counseling situation. You are there to pray for them.

Use Scripture as much as possible as you pray for their need. This lends authority and confidence to your prayers.

As much as possible, look for ways to bless and encourage those who come for prayer. It is a wonderful thing to be given a blessing in prayer.

More intense prayer: When the situation warrants, an escort can accompany the person to the prayer room for additional prayer or appropriate counseling. For example, if someone needs financial help, the team should pray for the need and then ask a trained financial or benevolence person to help. Keep notes for referrals to staff or other counselors.

Open altars: Many churches announce that the altars are always open for prayer and make space for people to respond to the Holy Spirit when he moves upon their hearts. Perhaps the message they heard or the worship they are engaging in compels them to make some kind of a response, and they just need to deal with God. Some people feel burdened by sin and feel conviction to come to God right away rather than wait. Having a place to go is helpful in that moment.

Prayer from the Platform

Pastoral prayer: Make prayer purposeful, not perfunctory. Don't relegate prayer to opening and closing the service, praying for the offering, or providing the chance to move people and things onstage while the congregation's eyes are closed. Give prayer a significant role in a worship service. Possibilities include: praying for the needs of the church and congregation, praying for missionaries and nations, or praying for area congregations and their leaders by name. Pray also for current concerning issues in the community or nation.

Periodically consider bringing children up to the front to pray for them during the worship service. Imagine the impact on the hearts of young ones when they are prayed over by the leaders in their church!

When missionaries are visiting, or when a short-term missions team is headed out for ministry, bring them up to the front and ask people to lay hands on them and pray over them.

Answered prayer testimonies: Consider short live interviews or videos of what God is doing in answer to prayers

Corporate prayer: Break the congregation into groups to pray for one another or for others. Or perhaps people could text their prayer needs so their requests can be displayed on the screen for people to pray about. Encourage people to participate in some kind of prayer experience in different parts of the worship center for a few minutes during the service. Brainstorm other creative ways to allow the congregation to pray with and for one another during the worship service itself.

Prayer Room Praying During the Worship Service

Recruit a team to pray through the worship service from start to finish. Charles Spurgeon talked about the people sitting beneath his pulpit in the boiler room of the church praying earnestly for him and for his message. He credited their prayers for the power that came to his preaching.

If your church has only one service, consider recruiting rotating teams assigned to the prayer room one week each month.

If services are taped, those in the prayer room can watch the service later. Some say they feel more engaged praying for the service than if they were actually in the sanctuary. Some churches make audio or video of the service available to those in the prayer room so they can pray for the different elements of the service as they're happening.

Provide words to songs and text of the message ahead of time so that prayers can be offered for ears to hear and eyes to see.

Pray for the Holy Spirit to come in power, for people to respond to the gospel, and for hearts to be made right with the Father. Pray that lives will be changed and that many will choose to serve Christ and live their lives passionately for his kingdom.

Those in the prayer room can meet with anyone encountered by the altar prayer teams who needs more intense prayer or a referral for some other kind of help.

CHAPTER 11

INTERCESSORY PRAYER TEAMS:
HOW CAN I PRAY FOR YOU?

*E*very church will have a different way of praying for people before, during, or after worship services. Your prayer team can consider how to augment what the church is already doing or create opportunities for this to happen. Be sure to stay in touch with the staff person supervising the prayer ministry as you propose initiatives.

Intercessors for altar prayer teams don't necessarily need to also be on the Prayer Ministry Team, although some likely will be.

Quarterly training sessions are vital to equip these prayer teams with good methods and updated information. It's important to teach intercessors to take this assignment very seriously, because sometimes people being prayed for have life journeys and situations that may depend upon their experience with you in prayer.

Each intercessor should spend time with God before spending time praying with people. Praying with other intercessors before each service is also important. Pray for the Holy Spirit to guide their hearts and minds as they pray for others. They should pray for wisdom, knowledge, and discernment so that they can pray in wise and informed ways for the needs and situations of others. They should ask God to use them for the sake of his kingdom, and express their desire to bring him glory in this service of intercession. Ask God to bring people with needs to be prayed for, as so many will not step out without the prompting of the Holy Spirit.

When a Person Comes for Prayer . . .

- Warmly greet them to put them at ease. Ask, "How can I/we pray for you?" If the person begins launching into their life's story, intercessors should redirect the person by saying, "How would you like us to pray for you in this situation," or "What would you like us to ask God to do for you?" If this doesn't cause them to get to the point more quickly, they may need more time and help. The intercessor has two options: wait and listen to the whole story, or refer them to the prayer room so the intercessor can be free to speak to the next person waiting for prayer.

- Try not to spend the entire prayer time with one person. Welcome and pray for the person, leaving him or her with the encouragement that God has heard their request. Perhaps pray a blessing over them and then release them. You may wish to give all intercessors a sheet listing blessings, God's promises, and encouraging Scriptures to refer to and quote to the person seeking prayer.

- Train "back-up" intercessors to be ready to jump in if more are needed because of the number of individuals coming for prayer.

- Prayer teams should be identifiable in some way, even when they are standing up front. Perhaps a tag that says "Prayer Team." (Store in the church building; don't expect prayer team members to remember to bring them from home.)

- Train prayer teams how to respond when a person wants to know more about Jesus, wants to receive Christ, or has questions about baptism or church membership.

- If people want you to pray for something that goes against Scripture (i.e., "I want you to pray God will bring another person into my life because my spouse is not the one for me."), refer them to the prayer room. This person needs biblical counseling and just wants your prayer to be the stamp of approval for disobeying God.

- Sometimes people don't want prayer as much as they just want to be bailed out of a bad situation. If someone asks you to pray for a financial difficulty, do so. But also be ready to refer them to someone who can help them. The first step might be to talk with someone in the prayer room.

  The right counselor may be able to discern whether bad choices have caused the difficult situation. Or, if the need is beyond the person's control, the counselor can point him or her to help available from the congregation or in the community. A list of such resources should be available in the prayer room, if not with every intercessor.

- Any situation involving child abuse must be reported, first to a church leader, and then to proper authorities. Every intercessor needs to know the proper procedure for this. If adult abuse is reported, follow up to help the person find counseling or a safe house.

- Intercessors should complete an information card for each person seeking prayer. Ask if the need can be added to the prayer chain and record that on the card. Initials can be used if necessary. Use these cards to report to leaders when a person wants more information about baptism, church membership, or finding connections in the church body. If someone accepts Christ, they should receive information about baptism and/or next steps from someone in the very near future.

Prayer Room Intercessors

If you have a functioning prayer room, it is a best practice to have at least two people available, in case someone being prayed for in the worship service has a deeper need that can't be handled by the altar prayer team for some reason. For example, if someone needs to be referred for counseling or services, all of this information should be accessible in the prayer room and available to distribute. Also, if deeper, more in-depth time is needed in prayer, it is best to take the person to the prayer room to free up the altar prayer team to pray with more people who may be waiting.

If you are fortunate enough to have a trained counselor available, this person could be accessible through a text or page while they are in the worship service.

Prayer Room Escort

If possible, recruit a friendly, reassuring person who will be available to escort people to the prayer room for more intense prayer or to talk with a counselor about other services. This person should be visible and accessible to the altar prayer teams. Develop a workable system for how this transition should best take place.

CHAPTER 12

INTEGRATING PRAYER INTO CHURCH LIFE AND MINISTRY

*T*here is so much more to the ministry of prayer than events and programs! The more your team can, with the blessing of leadership, "infiltrate" other areas of church life, the more your church will be saturated with prayer! Prayer will become part of the DNA of your body of believers, and you will step closer to becoming a house of prayer for all nations!

Here are some ways to embed prayer into the normal activity of your church.

Remember to ask God where you should start. Beware of getting burned out by trying to do too much at once.

Bringing Prayer into Leadership and Staff Meetings

You have been given the responsibility to help build prayer into every aspect of church life—even among church leaders! Make an appointment with your pastor or the leader to whom your team is accountable and ask to talk about prayer in your church. Don't be afraid to ask what prayer looks like in staff and leadership meetings. If they generally only open and close in prayer, graciously and humbly challenge them to go deeper. Consider giving your pastors the book *With One Accord in One Place*, by Armin Gesswein (see bibliography), which is a short study and challenge to church leaders about prayer in the book of Acts.

Praying for Leaders

Ask your pastoral staff and leaders how you can be praying for them. Invite them into any intercessory prayer meetings that may happen in the church building during the week so they can be prayed for.

Worship/Creative Arts/Technology

When this team commits to praying with and for one another, their prayer leadership will grow stronger. Ask them how to pray for the individuals on their team and for their team's ministry. The devil would like nothing better than to mess with the worship of God.

Small Group Prayer/Sunday School Prayer

Consider a training time for these leaders to help them understand the importance of leading people into the presence of God in prayer.

Perhaps training them to pray at the beginning of their time together would put the focus on the Father and not just on the lesson. It doesn't have to be a long time, but enough to start stretching people beyond the list of health needs only. However, you can certainly pray for those things too! Here are some possibilities:

- Prayers of worship - Read Psalm 145 to prime their hearts and then ask people to call out, "Lord, you are_____ (rich in love, slow to anger, merciful, good to all, righteous in all Your ways, etc.).
- Pray for church staff and leadership.
- Pray for unity in the body in your congregation and the church at large.
- Pray for spiritual awakening in our nation and for government leaders locally through nationally.

- If there are any deep needs in your midst, stop and pray for that person right then!
- Bless one another in prayer. (See BLESS, in Chapter 8.)

Children/Youth Ministry

Ask how to pray for the pastors and staff who lead the kids. Children need a different level of instruction, so check out the resource on praying with and for children in this book.

Women's Ministry

Ask the leaders if you can begin a conversation about how to make prayer more visible and prevalent in women's ministry. Maybe your team could offer prayer training for women's groups. Encourage leaders to pray together as they plan, asking for God's guidance and wisdom.

Encourage women to find prayer partners or to create intercessory prayer groups that focus on a variety of topics, such as missions, government, families, lost loved ones, school children, college students, or your city's first responders. The following resources will help them.

- Praying for government (Intercessors for America: https://www.ifapray.org)
- Praying for school kids and college students (Moms in Prayer: https://www.momsinprayer.org)
- Praying for police (Shield a Badge - http://www.shield-a-badge.org)

Men's Ministry

Women's groups will naturally pray more in most circumstances. Men must be led into prayer. The leader of men's ministry must recognize this and be willing to teach prayer to men. Many men will openly admit that they don't know how to pray well. The answer to this is to teach it in small steps so they can grow in prayer.

Jesus, and the men who were his first followers, were men of prayer. The Apostles in Acts 6:4 expressed their belief that they must give themselves to prayer and the ministry of the Word. This then, becomes a model for men today as they follow the Lord.

Several practical tips for infusing prayer into the men's ministry of a local church:

- Every meeting should have not only a prayer time, but also a short teaching on one practical aspect of prayer.
- Challenge the men to grow in prayer to the point where they can lead their family in prayer.
- Develop a men's prayer list that should always include praying for their pastor, their church, and their family.
- Emphasize the spiritual warfare aspect of prayer and challenge them to be real warriors in this area.

Missions Ministry

Keep the names, faces, and needs of your church's missionaries and supported ministries front and center with the congregation for the purpose of prayer. Here are two ideas:

Each Sunday, display a picture of one family or the people who run a particular mission organization. Have the missions team gather prayer requests and praises from them ahead of time and include those on the display as well. Or have missionaries send a two-minute video prayer update.

Have the children in the church make missionary prayer notebooks that have pictures, prayer requests, and information about the people these missionaries are trying to reach for Jesus or serve in some way. They can pray as a class, in groups, or at home—however this is structured by teachers.

You will be surprised how these kids will want to communicate with, earnestly pray for, and perhaps even serve these missionary families.

Have at least one or two prayer experiences each year to focus on the missions of the church. Sign cards from everyone who came to the prayer time and send them to the missionaries saying they've been prayed for.

Encourage the families in your congregation to adopt one of the foreign missions organizations (although other organizations can certainly be prayed for as well...try developing prayer guides for each) for prayer each month, or for an entire year. Give them short prayer guides, perhaps based on the BLESS acronym found in Chapter 8.

Facilities Prayer

If you have a company that cleans, or people who are outside of your church family, begin to pray for them and let them know you are praying. Ask them how you can be praying for them and their families. Accompany your prayers with acts of kindness: notes of appreciation, cookies, or asking about their families.

For those maintenance and cleaning people who are believers, here are some simple ways to train them to pray as they work, if they don't already.

Ask each worker to:
- Recognize their worth and value in Christ as they serve in this way and to thank him for the opportunity and ability to work and make an important difference.
- Know that this is more than a job—it's a ministry.
- See their work through the eyes of Jesus, who considered himself a servant and in humility did the work the Father gave him to do.

- Practice the presence of Christ in each moment they are cleaning—being aware of his presence with each step and sensing his pleasure in their service.
- Begin to pray as they enter a new space: "Father, I bless those who will use this space with Your peace. Help them to sense Your nearness. Give them hope and joy and a deeper knowledge of who You are!" (or something similar). (Perhaps someone on the prayer ministry team could prepare several different scriptures, blessings, or prayers that could be prayed over each room or area. Give the workers a list to choose from as they go from space to space.)
- Thank the Lord when they are finished for the opportunity to do the work that many others would or could not do.
- Ask the Lord to bless the work of their hands and dedicate it to the work of his kingdom.

This may seem like a strange thing to ask janitorial/maintenance people to do, but it will likely bless them and keep them mindful that Christ sees their work as an act of humility and service.

Praying through the Church Calendar

Assign one prayer team member to get a copy of the church calendar each month, making sure it's up-to-date and complete. Your team or other intercessors can focus on each day's events. Covering all activities in prayer can maximize their effectiveness by inviting God's presence, protection, and power! You can go a step further and seek out the organizers or people taking the lead and ask for specific requests. Gather a group to intercede prior to the event and perhaps even during the event. And be sure staff retreats and leadership meetings are always thoroughly covered in prayer.

CHAPTER 13

HOW TO SET UP, USE, AND SUSTAIN
A PRAYER ROOM

*"Prayer without action grows into powerless pietism, and
action without prayer degenerates into questionable
manipulation."* — **Henri Nouwen**

It's Important!

Providing a dedicated space for prayer is important, because it shows that church leaders value prayer enough to create space for it. It is a place where pastors, staff, leaders, and others can pray during the week as well as on Sundays. It is a special place for intercessors to come together to meet with God.

Your Prayer Room

Be intentional. Find a space that will be used for NO purpose other than prayer. Sharing space makes it look as if prayer is on the level with storage.

Be purposeful. Make sure the prayer room is more than a nice room with nice furniture and nice art. It is a war room! Make it look that way! Perhaps put up maps of the city, county, state, nation, and world. Have prayer guides and journals, Bibles, tissues, a keyboard for worship, and anointing oil. The room should look and function like God's business is being carried out there. It

settings. There are several different postures used by praying people in the Bible:

- **Standing** (Nehemiah 9:5; Mark 11:25; Luke 18:13) demonstrates respect and honor. It is also a way to signal to God that you are open and ready to receive His instructions.

- **Sitting** (1 Chronicles 17:16-27) is a posture of rest and can be a signal for waiting upon God.

- **Kneeling** (1 Kings 8:54; Ezra 9:5; Luke 22:41; Acts 9:40) indicates complete surrender. "Not my will but yours be done." It is often used to show repentance and humility.

- **Bowing** (Exodus 34:8; Psalm 72:11; Nehemiah 8:6) is another posture of humility. It also indicates honor and deep respect.

- **Lying prostrate** (Joshua 7:6; Ezra 10:1; Matthew 26:39; Mark 14:35) shows awe for the holiness of God, deep repentance, and crying out to God in brokenness.

- **Uplifted hands** (2 Chronicles 6:12-13; 1 Timothy 2:8) indicate praise and worship. This can also be a posture of surrender.

- **Walking** (2 Kings 4:35) is often a good way to focus on one's prayers even more intently and also for praying in the midst of spiritual warfare. It's hard to sit and do battle!

Encourage people to use whatever posture seems right to them in the moment without being concerned about the others in the room. Their prayers are to God, not to those around them. Try giving people opportunities to practice different postures together in a group so that individuals can become more comfortable with them.

Praying without Ceasing

Help people obey the exhortation of 1 Thessalonians 5:17: "Pray without ceasing." This is prayer that develops awareness of Christ's presence throughout our day and in all of our activities, conversations, and duties. Recognizing his presence in every aspect of our day is a process that will take time and practice. Teaching people to use "prayer triggers" will help in this. A prayer trigger is an activity, place, or situation that will prompt them to pray. For example, people can train themselves to pray whenever they are stuck in a line waiting, when they are doing mundane chores around the house, or when they come to a stop light.

Praying Scripture

Teaching people how to pray the Word of God will help many people grow in their prayer lives. Here are some of the benefits:

- People will learn that *the Bible is the best prayer manual* to use, and that it can continually be our "tent of meeting" with God.
- This is probably the best way to *help reluctant pray-ers learn how to pray out loud.*
- It will give *fresh vocabulary* to those who are stuck about how to pray.
- It will teach people *how to pray the will of God*. Since the Word of God is the truth of God, people will always be able to pray the truth!
- It will allow the *kingdom purposes of God* to be prayed and acted upon!
- It will help people *memorize the Word of God* as they begin to pray it back to him!

Training

Here are just a few ways to train people how to pray Scripture.

Praising God. Read Psalm 145 together and then ask, "What are all of the attributes of God you can find in this Psalm?" Have them write these down. Then, show them how to pray these attributes back to God saying, "Lord, you are_____!"

Blessings. There are many ways to use this wonderful Scriptural prayer practice. People can pray for family members, friends, missionaries, or pastors using these blessings. Pray them out loud, write them, e-mail, text, or speak them over the phone.

Sample Scriptural Blessings (there are MANY others):

- "The Lord bless you and keep you; the Lord make his face shine on you and be gracious to you; the Lord turn his face toward you and give you peace" (Numbers 6:24-26).
- "May the Lord direct your hearts into God's love and Christ's perseverance" (2 Thessalonians 3:5).
- "Now may the Lord of peace himself give you peace at all times and in every way. The Lord be with all of you" (2 Thessalonians 3:16).
- "May the God of hope fill you with all joy and peace as you trust in him so that you may overflow with hope by the power of the Holy Spirit" (Romans 15:13).
- "May the grace of the Lord Jesus Christ, and the love of God, and the fellowship of the Holy Spirit be with you all" (2 Corinthians 13:14).
- "May our Lord Jesus Christ himself and God our Father, who loved us and by His grace gave us eternal encouragement and good hope, encourage your hearts and strengthen you in every good deed and word" (2 Thessalonians 2:16-17).

Examples

- Place your hand on someone to pray a blessing over them. This can be a prayer directed to the Father or a declaration of blessing directed to the person. Here are two examples using Romans 15:13.
- Prayer of blessing directed to God on behalf of another: "God of hope, please fill my son with all joy and peace as he trusts in you so that he may overflow with hope by the power of the Holy Spirit! In the name of Jesus I ask it! Amen."
- Prayer of blessing for someone as you look at them, placing your hand on them: "Bill, may the God of hope fill you with all joy and peace as you trust in him so that you may overflow with hope by the power of the Holy Spirit!"
- This is a beautiful practice for any kind of celebration: birthdays, graduations, retirement, moving, wedding, or baby showers. Place the person(s) of honor in the middle of the room and lay hands on them. Or have people write out blessings to put in a special book for them.
- Suggest to church leaders that the children of the church occasionally be invited to come to the front of the church during a worship service. Have elders and parents lay hands on them and pray blessings over them using the Word of God.

Prayer Walking (Praying On-site with Insight)

Take the ministry of prayer to neighborhoods, businesses, schools, government buildings, or whole zip codes. It is, very simply, walking and praying with your eyes open. It is so simple that everyone can do it. Those unable to walk can ride a wheelchair. If the neighborhood is dangerous, people can prayer drive!

Here are some easy steps to train people how to prayer walk:

- *Decide who will go.* Individuals can pray as they walk for exercise or walk the dog. Whole families might choose to go on a prayer walk together. Groups can walk; the most effective number in a group is between two and four.

- *Decide where you will go.* Prayer walk neighborhoods close to the church building, asking God to draw unbelievers to your congregation. This may lead to other neighborhood outreaches: door-to-door calling, neighborhood carnivals, or a backyard VBS. But first, prepare the ground in prayer.

Prayer walk around school buildings, businesses, or government headquarters, asking God to change the spiritual climate in your community.

Pray for the unity of believers in your community by prayer walking around various church buildings, asking for God's peace, blessing, and presence to fall upon them. Ask him to show you ways you can serve the other churches and come together to serve your community.

- *Decide what to pray about.* Depending on your area and focus, give people prompts from scripture for their prayers. Perhaps you would begin with Psalm 23 or 1 Timothy 2:1-7. Or pray biblical promises as you walk. Don't carry Bibles and draw attention to yourselves. Perhaps have a printed sheet of suggested scriptures to pray.

- *Debrief afterwards.* Share stories and experiences. Ask if anyone could see ways the church or group could become the answer to prayers that were prayed, as in acts of kindness or service. Is the Holy Spirit prompting you to do something about a situation you encountered?

Decide whether to prayer walk in the same area again. If not, where should the group prayer walk next?

Listening Prayer

Alvin Vander Griend has very good definition of prayer: "Prayer is the conversational part of the most important love relationship in our lives, our relationship with the Father, Son, and Holy Spirit." Unfortunately, God's people usually do all of the talking and don't allow God to get a word in edgewise.

Teaching people how to be sensitive to the Holy Spirit and how to listen for and hear the voice of God is so important. The best context for listening is in silence and solitude; however, this atmosphere can also be cultivated in a corporate setting. Distractions such as cell phones should be removed. Learning to listen to God can remind people that prayer is a two-way conversation, and that sometimes we are so talkative that God is unable to respond or initiate conversation with us.

Many people are afraid to try listening prayer because they feel God may not speak. Practicing listening prayer builds faith. As God sees you are serious and want to hear from him, you will begin to hear.

King David spent much time listening to God: "My soul waits in silence for God only" (Psalm 62:1 NASB); "My soul thirsts for God, for the living God. When can I go and meet with God?" (Psalm 42:2).

Ways to Be Still and Know

- One of the best ways to train people in listening prayer is to read a short passage of Scripture and meditate on it in silence. Ask God to speak to hearts. A very short but important verse to begin with is Psalm 46:10. "Be still and know that I am (He is) God." Then, go to other Scriptures that speak to your heart. Ask God to speak.

- Have people get into a comfortable posture for listening. Also, having paper and something to write with is important when distracting thoughts such as, "What do I need at the grocery store?" come into one's head. Instruct people to quickly write down the distracting thought to come back to later.

- Spend time in his creation and see what God may say to you through it.

- After a period of time, ask people what they believe they may have heard, if anything. Or, have them write down or journal what they may have heard. Having pen and paper at hand gives people expectancy to hear from God.

Remind them that it's perfectly okay if they didn't "hear" anything. Sometimes it is more important just to be still and know he is God than to hear something.

How Do We Know What God Has Said?

Teach people to ask these questions about anything they believe they've heard from God:

- Does it agree with the Word of God? Scripture is our authority, and God will never contradict what he has already said (Proverbs 30:5-6).

- Was it a very clear word or just an impression? Sometimes God wants to have us know that we are loved and cared for by him. No other words may come other than this general impression from the Father.

- Does what you heard exalt Jesus? (John 16:14).
- Do other mature believers confirm what you heard? We are all fallible, and it is important to ask others to help us confirm what we believe we heard (Proverbs 20:18; Proverbs 15:22).
- Does God himself confirm his word? (Isaiah 55:11; Deuteronomy 18:21-22).

Listening prayer is not easy, but it is important. Sometimes we can miss opportunities for service or instructions that will advance the kingdom of God, heal a relationship, or solve a problem, because we are too busy talking and never stop to listen to the voice of our Creator.

Prayer Stations

Prayer stations can be used in so many different contexts; however, they are most effective during extended seasons of prayer, such as a 24-hour prayer vigil or a weeklong prayer emphasis. Design stations that can be used by a wide variety of ages, or design some special prayer stations for children to meet with God.

Search "Prayer Stations" on Pinterest for many great ideas. Gather a team of creative people who will pray about what kinds of stations to provide. Here are some ideas:

Use All Four Walls

In their book *Red Moon Rising,* Peter Greig and Dave Roberts make the following suggestion for devoting each wall of your prayer room to a different type of prayer.

Confession Wall: Perhaps a kneeling bench with a Bible open to Psalm 51, a basin with water and towels so people can wash one another's feet—offering and extending forgiveness to one another—or perhaps a fake fire (bricks, a fan, and orange streamers) to represent the presence of the Holy Spirit. Leave instructions so people know how to engage the space.

Worship Wall: Here is a place to offer gratitude and honor to the Lord. Perhaps base this station on Psalm 95:1-7, 1 Chronicles 16:29, Psalm 29:2, or Psalm 96:9—all of which say, "Worship the Lord in the splendor of his holiness." Provide a small tent where people can crawl in and worship privately. Or provide a space with the names of God and their meanings written in calligraphy where people can sit in a comfortable chair and meditate on all that God is.

Wailing Wall: Here is a place to write prayer requests and pray for other people's requests. Provide butcher paper with markers and pens. (Be careful on painted walls so that markers don't bleed through.) Maybe have a small water fountain where people can write the names of lost family and friends on rocks or craft jewels, pray over them, and place them in the water as an offering to God. Others can pick up the rocks and pray over them too.

World Wall: This wall is focused completely on the kingdom of God. Make prayer stations that utilize maps of your city, county, state, nation, and the world. Have a small hut for children with pictures of missionaries to pray for. There can be a place to pray for other churches, government officials, schools, and the needs of the nation.

Use Your Creativity

Have an art station for people to draw their prayers to the Lord. Provide all kinds of paper, paint, markers, crayons, chalk, clay, and lots of paper towels. Protect the floor and immediate area around the art station. This is a wonderful opportunity for people who can't express themselves with words to create their own prayers, or for children to draw their prayers to the Lord.

Provide a variety of worship music at one or two stations. Consider providing headphones.

Consider a guided prayer experience where people can listen to a podcast or recording and walk through the prayer stations getting instructions and inspiration.

Use a topical approach. Create stations that focus on the missions of the church, the community, the pastors and staff, schools, and government. Have one main theme and change stations from time to time to keep people interested.

Equip the room well. Have plenty of Bibles, journals, pens, tissues, floor pillows, lamps, and battery candles around the room. Perhaps leave a couple of journals already primed with Scriptural prayers so people add their prayers to it.

Practical Tips

It is important to have prayer team members available to guide people, make suggestions, keep supplies in stock, and clean up. They can be assigned rotating shifts.

Consider security, particularly if you are doing an all-night vigil.

CHAPTER 15

HOW TO LEAD A PRAYER MEETING

*L*eading a group before the throne of God is a serious responsibility. Take time to consider what is about to take place. Perhaps most importantly, the leader should pray about prayer. What does the Lord want to take place in your prayer meeting? In serious times of prayer, lives are changed and circumstances are altered.

Planning is Essential

Keep a clear focus. Everyone attending or planning to attend needs to know what will be prayed about. People are more inclined to come to something clearly defined rather than "Everybody come to the prayer meeting." So often, unplanned prayer meetings leave participants with a feeling of vagueness and sometimes wandering in their prayers.

If you don't have a specific need or direction for your prayer meeting, spend time seeking the Lord for what he may desire you to plan.

Stick to a time frame. Keeping prayer meetings to an hour is the best way to engage the majority of your congregation and keep them coming back; however, there may be other occasions when they can be extended to ninety minutes or even two hours, as long as the meeting is well-planned and will keep people engaged. If the prayer meeting lasts only 45 minutes instead of an hour that's perfectly okay; however, do everything you can to keep the time from going over. If you sense the Holy Spirit wants your prayer time to be able to go longer, you need to let people know they are free to leave at the appointed time, especially if they have children being cared for.

Clarify assignments. Be sure everyone leading some part of the meeting understands their specific assignment and how long it should take. Recruit a worship leader who will use music to help turn people's hearts to the Father, to play softly during each prayer segment, and to help bring each section of prayer to a close. Be sure to assign someone to cleanup, publicity, and childcare. If you're not including children in your prayer time, find people who will pray with children and teach them about prayer during your prayer times with the adults.

Gather materials. Once there is a specific focus (the nation, missions, church leaders, healing, or another), gather materials that will be used in your room to help people engage in prayer. You can use prayer stations, maps, photos—whatever fits your theme.

Have something for everyone. Keep each prayer section short. Try intergenerational experiences, tap as many senses as possible, and use a variety of prayer methods.

Maybe "prayer meeting" isn't the best name. How about Fresh Encounter or Prayer Experience. Your meeting will be different than the prayer meetings most have attended at other places.

The Prayer Experience/Fresh Encounter
Start and end on time. Otherwise people won't come back.

Welcome. Thank people for coming, tell them about the flow of the prayer meeting so they know what to expect, and put them at ease by giving them permission to pray at their level of comfort —either out loud or quietly or silently.

Give clear direction. Make sure everyone knows exactly what they are to do. For instance, if you are getting into groups, tell them how to do it: how many people should be in a group and how and where to gather in their groups. Otherwise, people will mill around in confusion. Never make assumptions. People will not automatically know what you want them to do—many will be nervous, and some might be afraid of what is going to happen. Remind people to give everyone a chance to pray and keep their prayers short.

Pay attention to your group. Either have a prayer team member in each group or walk around and drop in and out of the different groups. Watch for those who try to dominate the prayer time or have their own agenda. Remind the group before the next segment that they need to be sensitive to others and give everyone an opportunity to pray.

Closing each section of prayer. When time for group prayers is close to ending, give a quiet reminder to begin bringing their prayers to a close.

Begin to pray to close the section of prayer, or have music become louder so it is evident when each prayer time is coming to an end.

End well. At the conclusion of your prayer time, worship and then celebrate what God will do in response to their prayers. Remind people that Heaven is now astir with activity because of their prayers and thank them for coming. Invite them to the next prayer gathering and other opportunities to get involved in the church's prayer movement.

The Place of Worship and Word

One of the best ways to stay on purpose is to make sure that both worship and Word are a part of your prayer times. Worship songs, especially at the beginning, move the prayer time from being us-focused to God-focused. Make sure your group understands that singing is not just a warm-up for prayer, but is a critical part of your prayer time. Sometimes you might have a prayer meeting that is only songs of worship.

Using the Word of God as the foundation of your praying will bring clear focus and boldness to your gathering. When Scriptures are used to format and direct your prayers, there will be a far greater confidence that you are, indeed, praying according to the will of God.

Take Delight in the Privilege

Leading people before the Lord in prayer is a great privilege. It should bring you delight. Relax and enjoy what is happening—don't allow anxiety over the outcome burden you. Especially do not worry over the numbers of those attending. Most prayer meetings, even in very large churches, are small. But when the power of God is present, the numbers do not matter.

CHAPTER 16

FIVE SAMPLE PRAYER MEETING OUTLINES

*P*oor planning leads to prayer meeting problems. If the leader has not prepared and simply opens the meeting with, "What do we have to pray about today?" he or she will probably hear nothing but people's problems, most of them health-related. The prayers will be people-based and not God-focused.

Dynamic prayer meetings occur when leaders take the time to prayerfully prepare for the meeting. Carefully read the section on **How to Lead a Prayer Meeting,** and then consider the possibilities here. These outlines are just guidelines and starters to spark your creativity as you consider the needs and opportunities where you are.

Pray for Missions

Preparation
- Display maps of the nation and the world to show where your congregation's missionaries serve.
- Include photos of your missionaries with their names and people group or nation they serve. Include prayer requests you've received from the missionaries. Mount these on the wall with the maps, or distribute maps and photos among tables where people will sit to pray.
- Plan to seat about eight or ten around each table.

- Invite representatives from any local missions groups to come, such as a crisis pregnancy center or campus ministry. If any missionaries happen to be in town, of course, invite them too.
- Decide who will lead each section of the meeting. This can be one or several leaders.

Welcome. Thank people for coming and briefly, but clearly, explain the evening so everyone knows what to expect. Give people permission to pray at their own level of comfort, whether that is out loud or praying silently in agreement with others. If you will be breaking into groups, let them know how that will work.

Leader: Read Psalm 67 out loud as a prayer to the Lord.

Worship Team leads one or two songs of praise.

Leader: "May the peoples praise you, God; may all the peoples praise you." Invite people to shout out their praise to God. For example: "Lord, we praise you because..." You may wish to prime the pump with two or three people to get things started.

Close this section by asking the people to pray at their tables that true worship would cover the earth and that God's people, and soon all the peoples, would worship in spirit and truth.

Leader: Ask each person representing an organization or nation (those who are related to missionaries on the field can stand in for them) to stand. Invite people to gather around them and lay hands on them. Ask them to introduce themselves and to share one or two prayer requests. Have the groups pray for each ministry and each person standing. Close the prayer time when it seems most groups are finished. Remember to give them a reminder that the prayer time is coming to a close.

Leader: Now ask the groups around the table to pray for the missionaries and their requests that are not represented in the room. The photos and requests should be on the tables. Close the prayer time after a few minutes.

Leader: Ask people to choose a nation to pray for, and find it on one of the maps in the room. Read this verse: "The land yields its harvest; God, our God, blesses us" (Psalm 67:6).

As they lay their hands on the nations they've chosen, ask them to pray for God's ways to be known and for the land to yield a great harvest. They can pray out loud or silently. Close the prayer time after a few minutes.

Leader: "For you rule the people with equity and guide the nations of the earth" (v. 4). In small groups, ask what it would look like for God to rule as this passage declares. Then pray about what you have discussed. Close the prayer time after a few minutes.

Leader Declaration: What will be the result of our prayers? "So that your ways may be known on earth, your salvation among the nations. . . . May God bless us...so that all the ends of the earth will fear him" (vv. 2, 7). Ask each person to picture a world where all nations fear the Lord in reverent worship.

Worship: Close out with a song of worship that speaks of the nations!

Pray in the Midst of Spiritual Warfare

Worship and Welcome: Explain why we are here and what we will do. Everyone should have access to Bibles.

Leader reads Ephesians 6:10-18 and gives a brief explanation of spiritual warfare:

- Life is war.
- Our enemy is not flesh and blood.
- We have armor to protect us.
- Scripture is the offensive piece of the armor.
- The teaching is set in the context of prayer.

Leader reads this quote from John Piper: "Until we know that life is war, we won't know what prayer is for."

Leader: Affirm the victory that Christ has already won and pray from this place of victory. Read, "Then the end will come, when he hands over the kingdom to God the Father after he has destroyed all dominion, authority and power. For he must reign until he has put all his enemies under his feet" (1 Corinthians 15:24-25).

Offer a prayer of thanksgiving for the victory of Christ that we walk in.

Leader: "Put on the full armor of God so that you can take your stand against the devil's schemes" (Ephesians 6:11).

Say: We are going to put on the armor together! Something God commands us to do. Ask everyone to stand and go through putting on the bodily armor, saying this together repeating after the leader:

Lord, I put on the helmet of salvation.

I put on the breastplate of righteousness.

I put on the belt of truth.

I put on the shoes of the gospel of peace.

I take up the shield of faith to extinguish the flaming arrows of the enemy.

I take up the sword of the Spirit, Your Word!

Leader: Have people get into groups of four or six. Say: "We are going to pray the victory of Christ in our homes." "Have you not put a hedge around him and his household and everything he has?" (Job 1:8).

Use Psalm 91 as a basis for your prayers and pray for victory over the enemy for our homes and over our family members.

Leader: "His intent was that now, through the church, the manifold wisdom of God should be made known to the rulers and authorities in the heavenly realms" (Ephesians 3:10).

Have church leaders stand up and ask people to gather around them. Pray the victory of Christ in his church.

Leader: "Blessed is the nation whose God is the Lord" (Psalm 33:12). Get in groups and pray the victory of Christ in our nation!

Leader: "Therefore, God exalted him to the highest place and gave him the name that is above every name, that at the name of Jesus every knee should bow, in heaven and on earth and under the earth, and every tongue confess that Jesus Christ is Lord, to the glory of God the Father" (Philippians 2:9-11). Let's worship the One who rules over all things!

Worship: Close with two upbeat worship songs, declaring the defeat of the enemy.

Pray for Revival

For this meeting, everyone needs a Bible or at least a copy of Psalm 107. If you're using sound amplification, provide a microphone members of the group can use as indicated below.

Group people into circles of four or six and reassure them that no one will be asked to pray out loud who is uncomfortable doing so.

Leader: Read Psalm 107 or have another do so. Say, "This Psalm begins and ends with the Lord. In between it marks the way the Lord steps into the lives of his people when they get serious about calling on his name. In verse 2, we read: 'Let the redeemed of the Lord tell their story.' Stories encourage revival! In this Psalm, four groups tell their stories. We are going to pray through each of these stories."

The key to God's response in each story was the crying out of God's people. If we want to see God move in our midst, there must be a serious crying out of the church.

Story 1: Lord, we have wandered...

Leader: Read "Some wandered in the desert wastelands, finding no way to a city where they could settle. They were hungry and thirsty, and their lives ebbed away" (vv. 4-6).

"We are a wandering church that has lost its way. We are hungry and thirsty. We need wisdom and the guidance of the Holy Spirit."

"Then they cried out to the Lord in their trouble" (v. 6). In your small groups, cry out on behalf of the church, asking for the guidance of the Holy Spirit. Ask him for the wisdom he has promised if we will ask to find our way once again. Bring the prayer time to a close after a few minutes.

Leader: Ask, "What is God's response to our crying out?" Refer them to the Psalm.

- He delivers us from our distress.
- He leads us by a straight way to provision, a place where our needs are met.
- He satisfies the thirsty and fills the hungry with good things.

Leader: Lead the group in unison to say the following response to God: "Lord, we give thanks to you for your unfailing love and your wonderful deeds for your people!

Story 2: Lord, we have rebelled against your Word.

Leader: Read verses 10-11. Pray, "Lord, we have been sitting in darkness and are in bondage because of our rebellion against the Word of God. We have been subject to bitter labor (labor that shows no fruitfulness or results)."

Read, "Then they cried out to the Lord in their trouble" (v. 13). In small groups, have each person share something they feel God is calling them to do that they are ignoring, unwilling to do, or afraid of doing. Pray for one another's situations. Pray prayers of repentance and share with God a desire to submit to his plans and purposes for you as revealed in his Word. Leader brings prayer time to a close.

Leader: Ask, "What is God's response to our crying out?" Refer them to the Psalm.

- He delivers us from our distress.
- He brings us out of darkness.
- He releases us from our bondage.

Leader: Lead the group to offer this response to God in unison: "Lord, we give thanks to you for your unfailing love and your wonderful deeds for your people!

Story 3: Lord, we have been suffering affliction as a consequence of foolish behavior.

Leader: Read verses 17-18. Say, "We, the Church, have been suffering because we do not confess our sins so that we can be healed. Confession, repentance, and healing are always tied together."

Read, "Then they cried to the Lord in their trouble" (v. 19). Ask everyone who is able to kneel or to get in a posture of humility. Ask people to call out sins of the church one by one. When they are done, lead in a prayer of corporate confession and repentance for these sins.

Leader: Ask, "What is God's response to our crying out?" Refer them to the Psalm.

- He saves us from our distress.
- He sends out His word to heal us.
- He rescues us from death.

Leader: Lead the group to offer this response to God in unison: "Lord, we give thanks to you for your unfailing love and your wonderful deeds for your people!" Say, "We sacrifice thank offerings and tell of His works with songs of joy" (v. 22).

Say, "Let's call out our thankfulness to him. Thank You, Lord for..."

Worship: Here is a good place for a song of joy and thankfulness to God.

Story 4: Lord, we have been afraid. We have seen your works and we are serving you. But when trouble comes our courage melts away.

Leader: Read verses 23-27

Say, "There is a spirit of timidity and passivity affecting the church today. We see God doing amazing things but don't trust him enough to believe he will do them in our lives. Let's respond by declarative praying! There is an open microphone up here. Come up as you feel led and speak out a verse or passage that declares God's overcoming power in the face of opposition!"

The leader may wish to begin have one or two others ready to step up and share a declaration to encourage others.

Quote, "In this world you will have trouble. But take heart! I have overcome the world" (John 16:33).

Leader: Ask, "What is God's response to our crying out? Refer them to the Psalm."

- He brings us out of our distress.
- He calms the storms.
- He brings us into a safe place.

Leader: Lead the group to offer this response to God in unison: "Lord, we give thanks to you for your unfailing love and your wonderful deeds for Your people!"

End with worship songs.

Pray for Healing

Worship and welcome. Explain the theme and purpose of your meeting. Begin with a song of worship.

Leader: Read this verse: "Jesus went through all the towns and villages, teaching in their synagogues, proclaiming the good news of the kingdom and healing every disease and sickness" (Matthew

9:35). Leader prays, thanking the Lord for the healing ministry of Jesus.

Leader: Read this verse: "The Lord sustains them on their sickbed and restores them from their bed of illness" (Psalm 41:3). Pray, asking the Lord to do today what his Word says he does regarding healing.

Leader: Group people into circles of four or six. Say, "Now we are going to pray for help from the Lord for physical healing."

Quote Psalm 30:2: "Lord my God, I called to you for help, and you healed me."

In small groups, invite people to share their physical problems or illnesses and then pray for one another to be healed. This will take most of your time. Close in prayer after it seems most people have had a chance to be prayed for.

Leader: Read James 5:13-16.

"Is anyone among you in trouble? Let them pray. Is anyone happy? Let them sing songs of praise. Is anyone among you sick? Let them call the elders of the church to pray over them and anoint them with oil in the name of the Lord. And the prayer offered in faith will make the sick person well; the Lord will raise them up. If they have sinned, they will be forgiven. Therefore confess your sins to each other and pray for each other so that you may be healed. The prayer of a righteous person is powerful and effective."

Ask pastors and church leaders to stand. Ask others to gather around them and lay hands on them.

Say, "Pray for your church leaders to respond in faith to the scriptural command to pray for the sick. Pray for yourselves that you might respond in the appropriate way when you are sick and ask your elders to pray for you!" Bring the prayer time to a close as you feel led.

Leader: Quote 3 John 1:2: "Dear friend, I pray that you may enjoy good health and that all may go well with you, even as your soul is getting along well."

Say: "In your small groups, pray this scriptural blessing for the person on your right, going around the circle."

Worship. End with at least one worship song.

Pray for Schools

This is a good focus prior to the beginning of a new school year!

Ahead of time: publicize that you will be praying for the schools in your community and that everyone is invited: teachers, administrators, students, parents, school board members, and all who are interested in praying for the schools in your community. You may wish to send out invitations to the schools so educators will know about the prayer time. Have sign-up sheets ready for people to volunteer to prayer walk your schools and school administration building(s). The invitation to do this will come at the end.

Give everyone the lists of scriptures mentioned for each section below so that they can use them in their prayer times.

Choose two or three people ahead of time who will pray over the schools in your district, touching on topics such as safety, nurturing environment, the encouragement of children, good discipline, and support of the community.

Worship and welcome. Explain the purpose of your meeting and offer a special welcome to community guests from your local school system. Begin with at least one worship song.

Leader: Read Micah 6:8. "He has shown you, O mortal, what is good. And what does the Lord require of you? To act justly and to love mercy and to walk humbly with your God."

Ask the people you have primed ahead of time to lead out in praying for the school environment in your community.

Prayer Focus: Teachers

Leader: Ask teachers to stand and have people gather around them to pray. Remember to invite homeschool parents to be a part of this group.

Read: "I will instruct you and teach you in the way you should go; I will counsel you with my loving eye on you" (Psalm 32:8).

Point out that God is the ultimate teacher.

Ask each teacher to give one brief prayer request to the people standing around them and then give a few minutes for people to pray. Here are some of the scriptures they can use in their prayers (which should be on the sheet you prepared ahead of time for them):

"Instruct the wise and they will be wiser still; teach the righteous and they will add to their learning" (Proverbs 9:9).

"Start children off on the way they should go, and even when they are old they will not turn from it" (Proverbs 22:6).

"Teach them his decrees and instructions, and show them the way they are to live and how they are to behave" (Exodus 18:20).

Prayer Focus: Administrators and School Board Members

Leader: Ask any administrators or school board members to stand and ask everyone else to gather around them to pray.

Read: "Peace I leave with you; my peace I give you. I do not give to you as the world gives. Do not let your hearts be troubled and do not be afraid" (John. 14:27).

Instruct people to pray for peace and protection over schools. Pray that schools will be filled with those who seek the peace that comes from Jesus. Pray for wisdom, the best curriculum, and courage in the face of opposition.

Close by reading, or asking a volunteer to read these verses: "In everything set them an example by doing what is good. In your teaching show integrity, seriousness and soundness of speech that cannot be condemned, so that those who oppose you may be ashamed because they have nothing bad to say about us" (Titus 2:7-8).

Prayer Focus: Students

Leader: Ask students to stand and invite everyone else to gather around them to pray.

Before the prayers, read this verse: "Have I not commanded you? Be strong and courageous. Do not be afraid; do not be discouraged, for the Lord your God will be with you wherever you go" (Joshua 1:9).

Pray for courage to face the pressure of schools, and for physical, emotional, and spiritual protection.

Then quote, or ask a volunteer to quote this verse: "Don't let anyone look down on you because you are young, but set an example for the believers in speech, in conduct, in love, in faith and in purity" (1 Timothy 4:12). Pray for students, and for everyone present, to be an example of what God desires. Ask for godly wisdom to be developed even as knowledge grows. Read, "And Jesus grew in wisdom and stature, and in favor with God and man" (Luke 2:52). Close prayer time.

Closing the Meeting

Leader: Thank everyone for coming and for caring about one another and for our schools, teachers, administrators, parents, and students. Encourage them to consider doing one or both of the following:

- Encourage the students to begin student-led prayer groups on their campus! More information is at claimyourcampus.com.
- Ask for people to sign up to prayer walk one or more of the schools in your community. Organize

a day of prayer walking around schools. This is best done on a weekend or evening or during the summer before school begins.

Pray a prayer of blessing over the gathering, such as Numbers 6:24-26.

Worship music as people exit.

CHAPTER 17

HOW TO PRAY FOR YOUR CHURCH, PASTOR, AND LEADERS

*T*his is perhaps the most important work of the prayer ministry team. Be sure to make this the focus, because if the enemy gets a foothold, the house of prayer for all nations could get blindsided, sidelined, or incredibly damaged.

Your team oversees the front lines of spiritual battle on behalf of the church, because if there is one thing the devil hates more than anything else, it's prayer. He knows it defeats him and he will go to great lengths to disrupt, distract, and damage those who practice it. Many of you have already experienced this, and know also that if the enemy can't get at you, he will go after your family and your ministry next. It is the same for church leaders. The enemy knows that if he can take down the pastor, his family, or a prominent church leader, he will win a great victory.

That said, be sure you are all diligent to pray for one another as a team, as well as your families. Recruit others to pray for your team also!

Below are some simple Scriptural ways to pray for the pastors and spiritual leaders in your church:

The Acts 6:4 Prayer

The apostles were told that some of the widows were being overlooked in the distribution of food. They determined that it wouldn't be right for them, as leaders, to give themselves to this responsibility, because they were called to give their attention to prayer and the ministry of the Word. Pray that your pastors and leaders would continually keep their focus on prayer and the ministry of the Word and give tasks that distract them from this focus to others.

Personal Life

Pray for pastors and leaders to . . .

- Seek first the kingdom of God (Matthew 6:33).
- Dig deeply into the Word of God with delight and enthusiasm (Psalm 1:1-3).
- Live out a satisfying and joyful lifestyle of prayer (1 Thessalonians 5:17).
- Have a deep desire to know Christ more intimately each day (Psalm 27:4; Philippians 3:10).
- Walk by the Spirit and demonstrate the fruit of the Spirit (Galatians 5:16, 22-23).
- Be transformed by the renewing of their minds day by day (Romans 12:2).
- Walk worthy of the calling they have received (Philippians 1:27).
- Do justice, love mercy, and walk humbly with God (Micah 6:8).
- Regularly get away with Jesus to quiet places for rest and restoration (Mark 6:31).

Family Life

- Pray for pastors and leaders who are married to treat their spouses in loving ways and pursue strong marriages (Ephesians 5:25).
- Pray for pastors and leaders who are fathers to be godly, dedicated, and loving (1 Timothy 3:4-5).

- Pray for the children of pastors and leaders to grow up in the fear of the Lord (Ephesians 6:4).
- Pray for pastors and leaders and their families to be protected from the attacks of the enemy (Ephesians 6:10-18).

Ministry Life

- Pray for your pastor to be faithful in preaching the word and applying it in applicable ways to the lives of the congregation (2 Timothy 4:1-2).
- Pray that pastors and leaders would preach Jesus Christ crucified (1 Corinthians 1:23; 2:2).
- Pray that pastors and leaders would continually pray for the congregation (Ephesians 1:16; 3:14-19).
- Pray that pastors and leaders would be disciplined, hard workers for the sake of the kingdom (Titus 1:8; Colossians 3:23).
- Pray for pastors and leaders to work diligently to handle the Word of truth correctly (2 Timothy 2:15).

There are obviously many more Scriptures that can be prayed over pastors and leaders, but this will give you an idea of where to start.

Praying for the Church

- Pray for a spirit of prayer to be poured out upon the congregation (Zechariah 12:10).
- Pray for the church to become a house of prayer for all nations (Isaiah 56:7; Mark 11:17).
- Pray for people to be filled with the knowledge of the will of God in all wisdom and spiritual understanding so that the people may live and

conduct their lives in a worthy manner, fruitful in every good work (Colossians 1:9-10).

- Pray for the congregation to stand fast in one spirit, striving together for the faith (Philippians 1:27).
- Pray that the people will set their minds on things above and not on the things of earth (Colossians 3:2).

Again, this list of Scriptures is just a beginning. Keep a list of the many Scriptures that can be applied to praying for the church!

CHAPTER 18

PRAYER REQUESTS

$\mathcal{H}$ere are some ideas for handling the prayer needs of your church.

Prayer Appointments

Schedule one night a week when a team of intercessors is available to pray with anyone who comes to the church building. It is important to have a team so that men can pray with men and women can pray for women. Otherwise recruit at least three people, with at least one of each gender. Your experience may tell you that you need more than two or three intercessors. Ask those coming for prayer if they would like their need to be shared with the prayer chain, the staff, or other intercessory groups. Devise a system for sharing such requests.

Prayer Request Box/Card/App/Text/Email/Website

Before, during, and after services, and throughout the entire week, there should always be ways for people to share their prayer requests.

Decide which method for gathering prayer requests will work best for your congregation. As the heading indicates, there are many possibilities. Choose one centralized place, and make sure you've done the following:

- Communicate—well and often—how people can make their requests known.

- Recruit one member of your prayer team to take the lead in gathering the requests.

Remember, there are different levels of sensitivity. Create a way for requesters to say how their requests are distributed: to the pastoral staff, the intercessory prayer team, or anyone on the prayer chain. Respect people's need for privacy. Guarantee that they can receive prayer without publicizing their request.

Train altar prayer teams, floating intercessors, and prayer room intercessors to ask the people they pray for if they would like others to pray over their request. Fill out a card with a name or initials so that this can take place, and so that you can follow up with each person you pray with or for.

Have prayer request cards in your bulletin, on pew seats or altars, or at the welcome center. The cards should invite people to leave their requests and tell them the follow-up their requests will receive. People should know they can be totally anonymous if they wish. The card should say where they can deposit it so they will be prayed for. Containers, boxes, or a slot in a door for these cards should be easy to find.

Always have a plan to pray for these requests. Someone should be assigned to read them immediately after the service so something urgent can be prayed for right away. Next, the plan may be that staff prays over them on Monday mornings and passes them along to an intercessory prayer team that meets in the morning or evening in the next day or two.

Prayer Chain (See Chapter 19)

PRAYER CHAINS

*P*rayer chains, as they existed in the past, are becoming obsolete, as the "pass it on" by telephone method has become less and less the preferred mode of getting requests out quickly and efficiently. Today there are many better options for getting prayer needs to intercessors in a timely manner.

Prayer apps. Ask someone on the prayer team to explore the options among the many prayer apps available today and suggest two or three that might be the best fit.

Email prayer chain. This works well if there is one centralized place for all of the requests and updates to go. One person should take the lead who has a passion to gather and follow-up on prayer requests. Perhaps the best idea is to have a prayer@nameofchurch. org address. This way, one person's email isn't inundated with all of the prayer requests and nothing gets lost. The requests can be posted on the app, printed on paper and placed in the welcome center or in the bulletin, or sent out as a group email to those who wish to receive the prayer requests this way. Be sure to follow up and share answered prayer and updates!

Phone. Best practice if you want to use this method is to have a central number people can call to leave a message. Instruct people to leave their name and number so you can call them back if clarification or updates are needed. The best use of the phone is to follow up on requests to see how God is answering prayer or to get updates.

Text. A group text can be sent; however, this can be problematic since every text goes to every person. Best practice for this method is to instruct people to respond only to the person who sent the text and not the entire group!

Printed Prayer Sheets. If you wish, or for those who are unable to access a cell phone or computer, have a printed sheet available upon request.

Password protected place on church website. This is another way people can access the prayer requests.

DOs and DON'Ts of Prayer Chains

DO have set guidelines about how the chain will work! Make these guidelines clear.

DON'T allow people to use the prayer chain as a way to pass along or spread gossip. Be sure everyone understands the confidentiality of every request.

DO verify that it is okay to use someone's name. If you don't have that verification, use initials or some other way to protect identity. People can pray without knowing who they are praying for. God knows.

DO verify the name of the person submitting the request and be sure they have permission to do so. Put the submitter's name in parentheses with the request so you can follow up with this person later to update.

DON'T allow anything on the prayer list that is graphic in nature or should be referred elsewhere. If you learn about abuse of any kind, you are required by law to report it—but not to put it on the prayer chain.

DO follow up! There should be one or two people whose task it is to call or email to verify how things are going.

DON'T leave requests up for days on end without an update or checking to see if the issue is improved, resolved, or needs more prayer.

DO have a method to determine how long a request will stay on the chain without an update.

DO share answered prayer! It builds faith, it encourages others to pray, it honors God when people praise him for his goodness, and it allows people to see how others trust even when God doesn't answer prayer the way they wanted or expected. Taking time to do this is key.

CHAPTER 20

PRAYER RETREATS

*W*hether it was to choose his apostles, or just to get away from the press of the crowds, Jesus often withdrew to quiet places for prayer. Once, he invited the apostles to go with him (Mark 6:31).

If Jesus and his earliest followers needed these times of retreat, we must assume we do too. But he left no model for us to follow. Jesus didn't tell us what he did during the times away. He gave no instructions for our retreats. So we have great freedom to shape our retreats in ways we believe will bring spiritual benefit and advance God's purposes.

Guidelines

The length is variable. You can have an individual mini-retreat of a few hours or several days. Your congregation or small group might find a good length of time is a Friday night through Saturday afternoon. Find what works.

Your purpose is variable. Sometimes it might be physical or spiritual exhaustion that leads you to withdraw for a season. Some find a retreat is for discovering a fresh vision for the future. Some retreats are solely for spiritual intimacy with the Lord. Try to stick to one purpose, rather than trying to cover too much with one retreat.

Get away. It's very difficult to have the retreat in your own home or at the church building. The distractions of the familiar can make a retreat difficult. Many find that enjoying a beautiful outdoor setting is helpful for retreat.

Bring your Bible, journal, and perhaps a devotional or worship music you enjoy.

Decide beforehand if this will be a time of fasting or whether you should bring food. The purpose of your retreat will often determine this.

If you are doing a group retreat, the leader must have a clear plan with definitive action steps and activities for the participants.

Avoid media. It is good to be without television. But it might be even more important to be without your phone and laptop. Focus on the Lord!

Slow down! Whether you have a few hours or a few days, the most important part of this time is to sit at the Lord's feet and enjoy his presence.

Include an extended season of prayer, guided by the Scriptures. Continue recording thoughts in your journal as you direct your heart toward God in praise, confession, petition, and supplication.

Scriptures to Use
- Psalm 23.
- "As the deer pants for streams of water, so my soul pants for you, my God. My soul thirsts for God, for the living God. When can I go and meet with God?"
- (Psalm 42:1-2).
- "Yes, my soul, find rest in God; my hope comes from him" (Psalm 62:5).
- "Then we will not turn away from you; revive us, and we will call on your name. Restore us, Lord God Almighty; make your face shine on us, that we may be saved" (Psalm 80:18-19).

- "Return to your rest, my soul, for the Lord has been good to you" (Psalm 116:7).
- "I will refresh the weary one and satisfy the faint" (Jeremiah 31:25).
- "Come to me, all you who are weary and burdened, and I will give you rest" (Matthew 11:28).

Guided Prayer Walk for a Personal or Group Retreat

- Do this outdoors, especially in a place with trails or enough space for people to spread out and be alone with God. Consider creating stations where people can sit, stand, or kneel as appropriate as they move from station to station.
- You can also do this indoors, or even at home.
- Copy the following guide for each person to use.

Personal Reflection Prayer Walk

Directions: You will need plenty of time, your Bible, and a journal or paper and pencil. Read each Scripture slowly, perhaps even more than once. Write in your own words what you sense the Lord is saying to you personally through the passage. Answer any questions after carefully examining your heart. Pray as the Lord leads, perhaps even journaling your prayer.

1. Scripture Reading: Romans 12:2

What areas of your life have been conformed to the pattern of this world? How does your mind need to be renewed by God? Pray for God's strength and help in these areas, and then commit to God a renewed mind and life conformed to the pattern of heaven.

2. Scripture Reading: Psalm 139:23-24

What anxious thoughts do you have? Consider writing them down in your journal. Do you give them over to the Lord only to grab them back and worry about them some more? Ask God to replace anxiousness with his perfect peace, and to help you to replace any "offensive ways" with a clean heart and a renewed spirit. If you have written down your "anxious thoughts," write down a replacement you'll choose for each of them.

3. Scripture Reading: James 1:26

What circumstances or people cause you to lose control of your tongue? Pray for strength to control your tongue, speaking only uplifting and encouraging words to those around you. Ask God to give you the ability to stay silent when necessary. Pray for the wisdom to admit and correct anything harmful you may have said this past week.

4. Scripture Reading: Luke 10:38-42

List the top five priorities in your life right now (not what you think they should be, but actually what you spend the most time doing). Are they as they should be? Pray for understanding and wisdom in setting God's priorities into your life. Ask God to help you to seek him first so all other areas of your life can fall into place according to his perfect plan for you (Philippians 2:13).

5. Scripture Reading: Philippians 4:11-13, 19

Have you learned to be content in all circumstances? Do you really trust God to meet all of your needs (emotional, physical, and spiritual)? Are you too busy with the "things" of this world? What do you need to bring before the Father and lay at his feet so you can have the peace that passes all understanding and be content no matter your circumstances? Spend time in prayer about these things.

6. Scripture Reading: Ephesians 3:17-19

Pray for your physical family and your church family. Think about the love of Jesus Christ and what he did for all of us—for you! Admit to yourself that you are important to God and an important part in his plan for the church and his kingdom. Ask him to show you (or confirm to you) what gifts he has given you for service to others (Philippians 1:6).

Thank the Father for his presence with you through this season of reflection and prayer.

CHAPTER 21

SEASONS OF PRAYER AND PRAYER VIGILS

*T*here are times in the life of every church when extended prayer times are called for, such as a need in the congregation, a crisis in the culture, or a problem our troubled world. Sometimes the Holy Spirit will stir up the need to pray in extraordinary ways for a certain season. This season may be for 24 hours, three days, a week, or even longer. It may be something you choose to do once or twice a year, once a month, or continuously.

Here are some ways to create space in your church for people to meet with God for an extended period of time:

The Prayer Room

Why is it important for everyone to come to a prayer room instead of praying at home? There are several answers to this question.

- First, Jesus sought out sacred spaces for time with the Father, and so should we.
- Second, many people cannot imagine how it is even possible to pray for an hour or more at a time. A prayer room offers a variety of ways to seek the face of God, helping people meet with him in ways that fit their temperament, learning styles, and personality. A prayer room is a good teacher: people learn new, fresh, and exciting ways to pray—ways they may never have experienced or

even considered before. It is also a place where families and couples, as well as individuals, can come to engage the God of the universe in a holy conversation, or to simply sit and listen to his voice. Your prayer room will have its own unique, Holy Spirit-led design and expression.

Planning Guidelines

Recruit a planning team. Assign a leader and recruit a team. You want a group of people with the gift mix of administration and organization, creativity and servanthood, as well as those who will cover this time in prayer. It is a good idea if your team involves high school and college-age students. They are creative and enthusiastic, and often they're the most willing to come pray in the middle of the night!

Determine your focus. What is the purpose of this season of prayer? Be sure everyone knows why they are being called take part in it.

Find a suitable room for your day or week of prayer. It can be an already established prayer room, or a completely different space set apart for this season of prayer. Take your team and pray through the room, dedicating and anointing it as you set it apart as a sacred space for the purposes of God. You may wish to do this again once everything is in place, but before beginning your day or week. Ask the Holy Spirit to meet with people in deeply personal ways as they seek him there, and that God will move in response to the prayers of his people.

Publicize. It is important for leaders to encourage participation from the pulpit. Make sure the vigil is announced in the church's printed publications and digital posts. Consider creating short videos, posters, email blasts, texts, and calendar reminders.

Sign people up. It's best to offer one-hour time slots and have ways to remind people (either text reminders or phone calls). Use whatever sign-up system your church uses for other activities.

Setting Up the Room

Make this prayer experience **family friendly** so that there is something for people of all ages. This is a wonderful way for families to engage God together.

Use lamps, floor pillows, plants—anything to make this sacred space an **inviting place** to come and spend time with God.

Think creatively to find ways to **engage people of all temperaments and preferences**. Have a wide variety of options that will leave people wanting more time with God than their hour. Develop prayer stations to provide auditory, visual, and tactile kinesthetic experiences. Art stations are an excellent way to help people express prayer through sculpting, painting, and drawing.

Use your walls. Choose a different focus for each wall. Prayer stations can be part of the wall as well as inside the room.

Provide Bibles, journals and pens, sticky notes, tissues, and communion supplies. Provide lots of opportunities for people to interact with God. Have someone put an entry or two into each journal to give people the idea. Journals are a good thing for gatekeepers and watchmen (see below) to point out as people come to the prayer space. People can write prayers, give testimonies about how God met them in the prayer room, or write meaningful Scripture. Sticky notes are great for short prayers to just stick up on a map, for instance. We recommend a station where communion is available. Brainstorm other needed supplies.

Staff the Prayer Room.

Provide a watchman and a gatekeeper. Recruit teams of two people to be available during the entire prayer vigil/season/

experience. Their job is to orient people to the prayer room, answer questions, keep supplies replenished, keep the room in order, and to pray if someone doesn't show up for an assigned shift. They can take two-hour or longer shifts.

Consider security issues. Arrange for people to get in and out of the building safely, perhaps through one designated unlocked door or by the use of a keypad. Make sure the parking lot is well lit at night. Consider recruiting security volunteers who will serve overnight, perhaps guarding the unlocked door and escorting people to and from their cars.

Consider recruiting people to read the Bible out loud in the church building during the season of prayer. They can get through the entire Bible in a week just taking turns non-stop. Prayer and reading the Word aloud—a powerful combo!

Watch for the Impact

People will be captivated by what God does in an hour and how fast it actually goes. When they have a good experience with prayer, they will come back and encourage others to participate the next time. Many have said they could never have imagined praying in such creative ways and want to do it over and over again. You will find that many will never pray the same again and will ask when the next season of prayer is going to be.

CHAPTER 22

PRAYING WITH AND FOR CHILDREN

"*A*nd he took the children in his arms, placed his hands on them and blessed them" (Mark 10:16).

"Jesus said, 'Let the little children come to me, and do not hinder them, for the kingdom of heaven belongs to such as these'" (Matthew 19:14).

"Through the praise of children and infants you have established a stronghold against your enemies, to silence the foe and the avenger" (Psalm 8:2).

Children are very precious to Jesus. He created his people to seek him and to listen to his voice and to pray his kingdom plans and purposes. Prayer ministry teams cannot simply focus on adults and leave the prayer movement for children to others. A house of prayer for all nations is intergenerational, hand in hand, ministering before the Lord together. It is important that the prayer ministry team engages with those who work with the young ones, coming alongside of them, praying for them and with them, and helping in every way possible. Encourage and support parents and grandparents who are struggling to pray with and for their children.

Today, many parents are so busy they have basically abdicated the responsibility for teaching their kids to pray and grow in Christ to the church. Many parents feel inadequate in their own prayer lives, so they don't feel qualified to train their own children to meet with God.

Perhaps the main action step for your team is to meet with those leading your children's ministries and talk about how you can come alongside of them as a resource. If they are open and willing, brainstorm some ways that prayer can become more integrated into the existing ministry.

Offer help and resources for training workers, parents, and even children, if you have the people on your team who can help with this. Perhaps it will mean finding other spiritually mature believers with a heart for kids to help train workers, parents, and children in prayer. Children need mentors in prayer, maybe their parents, but an adopted "grandparent" in the church can work well too.

Here are some key points to pray about:

1. Parents, grandparents, and children's workers need training in how to pray and how to pray with and for children.
2. Children and youth pastors need to be training their teachers and workers in prayer and how to create space for children to learn and grow in prayer.
3. Opportunities for kids to be involved in the ministry of prayer need to be developed and expanded.

Guidelines from Scripture

Here are some specific scriptural ways to pray for children and their families, and ways for parents to pray for their children:

*   That Jesus Christ be formed in our children (Galatians 4:19, Ephesians 5:1-2).
*   That our children—the seed of the righteous—will be delivered from the evil one (Matthew 6:13).
*   That our children will be taught by the Lord and their peace will be great (Isaiah 54:13).
*   That they will learn to discern good from evil and have a good conscience toward God (Hebrews 5:14, Psalm 34:14).

- That our children will be godly examples to others (1 Timothy 4:12).
- That God's laws will be in their minds and on their hearts (Hebrews 8:10).
  That they will choose companions who are wise— not fools, nor sexually immoral, nor drunkards, nor idolaters, nor slanderers, nor swindlers (Proverbs 13:20; 1 Corinthians 5:11).
- That they will remain sexually pure and keep themselves only for their spouses, asking God for his grace to keep such a commitment (Ephesians 5:3, 31-33).
- That they will honor their parents (Ephesians 6:1-3).
- That they will enjoy good health (Proverbs 3:7-8; 3 John 2).
- That they will have freedom from fear (Psalm 46:1-2; Isaiah 41:10).
- That they will be filled with joy (John 15:9-11).
- Pray blessings on them such as Numbers 6:24-26: "The Lord bless you and keep you; the Lord make his face shine on you and be gracious to you; the Lord turn his face toward you and give you peace."

The Church of NOW!

Children do not have junior Holy Spirits, but we often treat them as if they do. They are capable at very young ages of learning to seek God and listen to his voice. When this happens, they'll be well on their way to growing in their relationship with Jesus.

Children are not the church of tomorrow; they are the church of NOW! This is why we teach them to pray.

CHAPTER 23

DISCUSSION QUESTIONS

*U*se the following discussion questions as a prayer team in considering what God is doing, and what you're hoping he will still do, through your prayer ministry.

1. Look at the list of roles and functions for prayer ministry team members in Chapter 5. Circle two or three on that list you're already doing or you could see yourself doing and share your choices with your group. Does everyone agree that you have the gifts to fulfill those functions? Cross out two or three items you would not consider for yourself. Compare your crossed-out items. Is there an item crossed out by every member of the team? Pray together about how or whether your team should seek someone to fill that role.

2. How has your vision for the power of prayer grown because you've read this handbook? How has your view of the place of prayer in the church's life deepened?

3. The handbook says one purpose of a prayer ministry is "to raise the level of awareness, knowledge, and participation in prayer within the church." On a whiteboard or piece of paper, make a list of at least twenty ways your team can do this. Then agree as a group on the three items from your list you should tackle first.

4. Which prayer posture do you assume most often? Why? Which prayer posture feels most foreign or uncomfortable to you? Why? How would your personal prayers be enriched if you assumed a different posture from time to time? When or how could your team encourage church members to assume a variety of prayer postures?

5. List all the prayer initiatives your congregation has experienced in the last six months or year (whether or not these happened because of your team's ministry). How can your prayer team build on those initiatives for a greater or more effective emphasis in the coming year?

6. Since many Christians struggle with prayer, describe the struggles you have or have had with prayer. What has helped you to overcome those struggles? What does this tell you about how to help other Christians feel more confident praying?

7. The book emphasizes the importance of starting slow and staying flexible. If your group has been functioning a year or more, how have you followed this advice? When were you forced to back off a big plan and settle for something smaller? When were you led to try something different than you originally intended? What have you learned from these experiences?

8. Look at the list of qualifications of a prayer team member in Chapter 9. Share with your group the one qualification you feel you *least* possess. Does the team agree with your self-assessment? What is one step you can take to shore up this weakness?

9. Look again at all the possibilities described under "Prayer Practices to Help Train Your Church Body" (Chapter 14). Circle those your team or your church has already tried. Put a star beside one or two you believe would be good to try in the next year (maybe something new, maybe something you've already done). Share your ideas with your group and agree together on next steps.

10. When in the last month has prayer been more of a delight than a duty to you? When has it been more of a duty than a delight? What can you learn about prayer by praying even when it at first feels more like a duty?

CHAPTER 24

RESOURCES FOR FURTHER HELP AND STUDY

Classics on Prayer

Billheimer, Paul E. *Destined For The Throne.* Fort Washington, PA: Christian Literature Crusade, 1975.

Bounds, E.M. *Power Through Prayer.* Grand Rapids, MI: Baker Book House, 1972.

_____. *Essentials of Prayer.* New Kensington, PA: Whitaker House Publishers, 1994.

Lawrence, Brother. *The Practice of the Presence of God.* Westwood, NJ: Fleming H. Revell, 1965.

Mueller, George. *Answers to Prayer.* Chicago, IL: Moody Press, 1895.

Murray, Andrew. *The Ministry of Intercessory Prayer.* Minneapolis, MN: Bethany House, 1981.

_____. *With Christ in the School of Prayer.* Westwood, NJ: Fleming H. Revell, 1885.

Resources for a Praying Church

Church Prayer Leaders Network (CPLN). The Church Prayer Leaders Network is for anyone who desires to see his or her church make prayer foundational to its ministry. This site offers more than 700 ideas, articles, and training videos to help you or your church be more effective in prayer. https://www.prayerleader.com

Butts, David. *Forgotten Power: A Simple Theology For a Praying Church.* Terre Haute, IN: PrayerShop Publishing, 2015.

Butts, Kim. *The Praying Family: Creative Ways To Pray Together.* Chicago, IL: Moody Publishers, 2003.

Franklin, John. *And the Place was Shaken: How to Lead a Powerful Prayer Meeting.* Memphis, TN: Master Design, 1999.

Gesswein, Armin R. *With One Accord in One Place.* Terre Haute, IN: PrayerShop Publishing, 2014.

Graf, Jonathan and Lani Hinkle. eds. *My House Shall Be a House of Prayer.* Colorado Springs, CO: Pray! Books, 2001.

Higley, Sandra. *A Year of Prayer Events for Your Church.* Terre Haute, IN: PrayerShop Publishing, 2007.

Sacks, Cheryl. *The Prayer Saturated Church.* Colorado Springs, CO: NavPress, 2004.

Teykl, Terry. *Encounter: Blueprint for the House of Prayer.* Muncie, IN: Prayer Point Press, 1997.
_____. *Making Room to Pray: How to Start and Maintain a Prayer Room.* Muncie, IN: Prayer Point Press, 1993.

CHAPTER 25

THE NATIONAL PRAYER ACCORD

The National Prayer Accord was first issued during the First Great Awakening in the United States during the 1730s and '40s. This Prayer Accord is now reissued in this dark hour as a simple pattern of prayer we can embrace in unity—asking Jesus Christ to once again pour out his Spirit on the church.

In recognition of:
- Our absolute dependence on God.
- The moral and spiritual challenges facing our nation.
- Our national need for repentance and divine intervention.
- Our great hope for a general awakening to the lordship of Christ, the unity of his body, and the sovereignty of his kingdom.

We strongly urge all churches and all Christians of America to unite in seeking the face of God through prayer and fasting, persistently asking our Father to send revival to the church and spiritual awakening to our nation so that Christ's Great Commission might be fulfilled worldwide in our generation.

We resolve to promote as an ongoing Prayer Rhythm:
- Weekly—one-half to one hour of private or small group prayer.
- Monthly—one- to two-hour individual church prayer gatherings.

- Quarterly—one- to two-hour local, multiple-church prayer gatherings.
- Annually—the National Day of Prayer (first Thursday of May).

The Prayer Accord was adapted by Dr. Robert Bakke as a modern take on the Concert of Prayer 1742 (Scotland), and its 18th Century adaptations.

ABOUT THE CONTRIBUTORS

The Writers
David Butts, president of Harvest Prayer Ministries, travels and speaks about prayer all over the world. He is chairman of America's National Prayer Committee, and serves on the boards of several other prayer and evangelism ministries. This is one of many books about prayer he has written himself, or with his wife, Kim.

Kim Butts, vice president of Harvest Prayer Ministries, travels with her husband, conducting prayer seminars and as a prayer ministry consultant to churches. She has written several books about prayer and dozens of magazine articles, blog posts, and digital daily devotions.
See more about their ministries at harvestprayer.com

The General Editor
Mark A. Taylor served in a variety of editorial, marketing, and management roles in a Christian publishing career that spanned more than 40 years, including 14 years as editor and publisher of *Christian Standard* magazine. In retirement he continues to take on a variety of editing and writing tasks as well as traveling, gardening, teaching, and serving in his local church.

PRAYER NOTES AND REQUESTS

PRAYER NOTES AND REQUESTS

PRAYER NOTES AND REQUESTS

PRAYER NOTES AND REQUESTS

Names   Phone and Email

_____   _____

_____   _____

_____   _____

_____   _____

_____   _____

_____   _____

_____   _____

_____   _____

_____   _____